MAKE CHRISTMAS REAL

John Henson

authorHOUSE®

AuthorHouse™ UK Ltd.
1663 Liberty Drive
Bloomington, IN 47403 USA
www.authorhouse.co.uk
Phone: 0800.197.4150

Published by AuthorHouse   04/26/2014

ISBN: 978-1-4969-7894-3 (sc)
ISBN: 978-1-4969-7895-0 (hc)
ISBN: 978-1-4969-7896-7 (e)

CREDITS

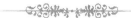

'John Henson and Ray Vincent have a Christmas present for you, and it just may be one of the best presents you ever receive. With skill and sensitivity the authors rescue Christmas from decades of greed and centuries of politically-motivated text to reveal the good news that so many never knew, and so many long to know today**. Read this book and experience a more loving celebration of 'God with us' than you ever thought possible.'**

Gregory Spayd,
Pastor serving St. Genevieve Parish, Corpus Christi, Texas

This is one of the finest—if not the finest—books I have read about the birth narratives of Jesus. Wow. Great job! Thanks.

Rance Darity, Graduate University of Kentucky,
Southern Baptist Theological Seminary, Mennonite Seminary.
An Anabaptist 'follower of Jesus'.

'Warning: if you love 'Christmas', reading this book could seriously spoil your festive joy. However, if even a little part of you has had it up to 'here' with festive cheer, consumerism, commercialism, and all the trappings of the 'traditional Christmas', then this book may well be exactly what you have been waiting for. **Creative, challenging, provocative, and scholarly, John Henson takes us on a journey that cuts through the Christmas traditions of the centuries, enabling us to hear afresh the radical story of the birth of Jesus.'**

Revd Dr Simon Woodman
Co-minister: Bloomsbury Central Baptist Church and
formerly tutor at Cardiff Baptist College, Wales.

"In Make Christmas Real, John Henson and Ray Vincent present us with the humanity of the Christmas story, and show us why it matters. Beyond the fundamentalism of Christianity today and the commercialism of our popular culture—Henson and Vincent speak truth—not mere facts—to our hearts. I cannot thank them enough for making christmas real to me again, and restoring true meaning to one of the most powerful, scandalous, and beautiful narratives of our shared faith. **May all who read this book be forever transformed by the love contained within its pages."**

Kevin Rodriquez, Administrator 'Progressives for America'.

Most people today are familiar with the Christmas story only at a 'primary school level' and so no wonder Christmas is thought of as 'for the kids', with no relevance for grown-ups who simply pick up the bills and the stress that surround the season! **In this thought provoking book, John and Ray, grounded in a faith that touches real people in the real world, invite the reader to expand their knowledge and imagination and to reflect on the message at the heart of the Christmas narratives**. I read this excellent book in one sitting (a fairly long sit for me)—but I am looking forward to a more leisurely, reflective reading in preparation for Christmases to come. A great present for anyone at any time of year!

Sue O'Hare, Methodist Minister, Caerphilly, Wales.

'John Henson's work is for a large part of the "religious" public a well-kept secret.'

Rowan Williams (Baron Williams of Oystermouth)
Archbishop of Canterbury 2002-2012

TABLE OF CONTENTS

SYNOPSIS

Introduction. The two major problems with regard to Christmas for Christians today—the spending bonanza and the misleading of the Church.

Chapter 1. Scripture, a book about people for people.

Chapter 2. New light on the relationship between Nazareth and Bethlehem and the manner of Jesus' birth.

Chapters 3 & 4. A fresh look at the visitors to the infant Jesus, and Herod.

Chapter 5. The theology of the fourth gospel made accessible to the average reader.

Chapters 6 & 7. Insights from J. K. Rowling & Sydney Carter

Chapters 8-14. Series of studies based on scripture stories of present-giving.

FOREWORD

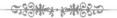

This book represents a compilation of two events, an Advent series of seven sermons preached alternately by Ray Vincent and John Henson at St. David's, Pontypridd, and John Henson's talks during another Advent given at the Othona Community in Dorset, England. At Othona one session was devoted to a sing-song, when John Henson's updated Christmas carols were all sung with great gusto. Some of these carols, to be found in *Wide Awake Worship*, are also included here. Ray and John hope a wider audience may be interested in what they think about Christmas.

Both John Henson and Ray Vincent are retired Baptist ministers who have ministered in ecumenical situations, and are members of St. David's, a Uniting and Inclusive church in Pontypridd, Wales. Ray is a chaplain at the University of South Wales. John continues to be involved in counselling and befriending. Ray is author of *Let the Bible be Itself* and *Chasing an Elusive God*, and John is responsible for *Good As New—a Radical Re-telling of the Scriptures*, *Other Temptations of Jesus*, *Other Communions of Jesus, Other Prayers of Jesus, The Gay Disciple, Bad Acts of the Apostles, Wide Awake Worship* and *Heaven and Hell and a Dish of Hot Potatoes.*

INTRODUCTION: WHAT DO YOU THINK OF IT SO FAR? (2011)

John Henson

'What you do think of it so far?' One of the catch phrases of the very funny Eric Morecambe. The answer was usually 'rubbish!' What if we ask this question of our experience of Christmas? What do we think of it so far? Let's be honest, we Christians have been worried about Christmas for many years now—ever since the end of world war austerity and rationing and all that. In those days, which few of us now can remember, Christmas was an opportunity to cheer us up in bad times. If we managed to have a chicken for Christmas dinner we were lucky. Stockings for most were still stockings rather than pillowslips, if you had them at all. The presents were few, often hand-made, or useful such as handkerchiefs, socks or a bar of soap. We entertained ourselves with party games or party pieces. Now Christmas has gone mad. It is a crazy shopping spree, which the shops cannot do without and which many shoppers cannot afford. Our country's economy would, apparently, take a nose dive if there were no Christmas booster. The flip side of this is that many families are getting more and more seriously in debt as a consequence. They cannot pay their mortgages and the Christmas over-spend does not help, nor do the divorces and family breakdowns that reach a peak at Christmas. Many people lose their homes due to re-possession. More and more booze is required to provide the merriment that people do not really feel inside. Is this the real picture? It is for far too many.

As Christians, we are not opposed, so we say, to people having a good time. Jesus came to bring 'life in all its fullness'. But we have to be concerned, and sorrowful, that year on year, Jesus is even more squeezed out than the year before. The life he came to bring is seemingly further away than ever. Look at the pretty lights that some households take so much trouble over. They do cheer up the dark days before Christmas, though they use a lot of energy and are yet another expense. Father Christmas is nearly always very prominently displayed. How often do we see a picture of Mary and Joseph and the baby? I enjoyed the Father Christmas experience when I was a child. It didn't worry me that my parents had told me a fib. I enjoyed it with my own children. But who is this overweight person, with his improbable attire and beard? The origin was Santa Claus—Saint Nicholas—still remembered and revered on the Continent. Saint Nicholas is usually depicted as a rather slender man. He left little presents on window sills for children too poor to have any. Our modern Santa, it seems has become a symbol of greed and over-indulgence, the very reverse of what Nicholas was about. The fat man in

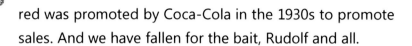

red was promoted by Coca-Cola in the 1930s to promote sales. And we have fallen for the bait, Rudolf and all.

Early in the new century we were given a little statistic which may mean something. More people were attending church at Christmas than in previous years. Was this a sign of weariness with it all and a hunger for something more satisfying? And are the numbers still keeping up? Maybe it's too early to tell. What we must ask ourselves as Christians is whether we are offering a real alternative to the superficial and sentimental glitz and spend, or are we just offering something on the same lines, but with a religious flavour? An alternative or rather an additional time out to the pantomime? The story of Santa Claus has been debased, indeed so turned around that it means very nearly the opposite of what was intended. Perhaps we have done the same with the Christmas story?

Perhaps it's just as well we don't see the crib scene in pretty lights on the walls of houses. Because there were no pretty lights at the first Christmas and it is not the reality of Christmas today. My own church had quite a debate at a church meeting over the size of the Christmas tree which appeared every year covered in lights and baubles and was getting bigger and bigger. It was voted to reduce the size.

We need to do a lot of work and a lot of hard thinking in our churches about the Christmas story. It's not just the semi-pagan things that we give prominence to, not just the pretty lights and Christmas trees and Father Christmas. We have twisted—and yes, we have *vulgarized* the Christmas story to such an extent that it comes over as no more real or meaningful than Father Christmas or Jack and the Beanstalk. It is one of many Christmas fairy stories and not the most popular.

It is not even true to what the Bible says, and very few Christians seem to care about that. They don't read their Bibles anyway, or do not read them very carefully. I had to read the Christmas stories very carefully when I worked on my new translation, 'Good As New'. It was time to translate the Greek correctly. Magi means 'magicians' not wise men, and very definitely not kings. The Magi were a weird, outlaw type of person, telling fortunes, selling lucky charms and so on. They should make us aware of a growing number of people today who are experimenting with a wide variety of spiritualities. They are people who have rejected the churches because they don't seem to them to be genuine. But this does not mean they have accepted the greedy and materialistic standards of our world today. They are green, concerned about the environment, healthy food and relaxation of mind and body. They seek an honest understanding of what it means to be a person and to have loving relationships. All the churches seem to do is to cling on to old ways, old ideas, and old traditions, without thinking deeply about the true meaning and its relationship to life today.

Then there is the problem with Christmas cards and their traditional presentation of Christmas. Was Jesus born in a stable as on our Christmas cards, or in a cave, as you will find if you visit Bethlehem? You will be shown the exact cave, and probably you will have to pay to go in. I went back to the text and to my Greek. I already knew what I would find, but I needed to check. We must keep doing that with scripture. When we think we know it, we don't.

There is no mention of the birth of Jesus being 'in the bleak mid-winter'. Susan Sparks at Madison Avenue Baptist Church New York, in 2011, led her people in celebrating Christmas in August in order to make the point. Most Christians today live in the southern hemisphere where 25th December is in the middle of summer. They also understand the picture of poverty and destitution that the Bible text indicates, which few of us in the north and west have experienced firsthand. There is a long tradition of putting in touches from our own imagination, and this is alright as long as we do not contradict the essence of the story. People like Francis of Assisi, and others in the Middle Ages introduced the animals. It is important to recognize their part in God's creation. Working animals were much closer to people in Francis' day. They often occupied the same living quarters. Francis also introduced carol singing, imagining there would have been boys and girls in Bethlehem who would have sung their songs to the baby Jesus. We still sing the same sort of carols. We have added to them, even some with modern words. But, by and large, we have depended on the imaginations of people of time past, instead of using our own imaginations. 'Little Lord Jesus no crying he makes'—that was somebody's rather pious imagination a couple of hundred years ago, and somebody who didn't know very much about babies. Must have been a man, old-style. Today we can allow ourselves to think of a baby crying, and dirty nappies.

If we only present the Christmas story to our visitors who only come to church at Christmas, in the old language and with old pictures, they may get a nice woozy feeling, as they might get by going to see *Sleeping Beauty* on ice, but they will not understand how the birth of Jesus connects with the life of the world today.

Folk frequently say, 'Christmas is for the children'. That shows how much our presentation has got it wrong. The Christmas story is for adults. There are some parts of it we can't talk about in front of the children, because it's X-certificate. It's about an unmarried mother giving birth in an inconvenient place; it's about asylum seekers and the homeless; it's about the fellowship of outcasts—queer folk and New Age travellers; it's about a cruel dictator and soldiers making an attack on a small community and slaughtering its children.

Don't let's blame the world for marginalizing Jesus. We've helped with the process, and we are still helping. Unless we go over the story again, making it true for ourselves,

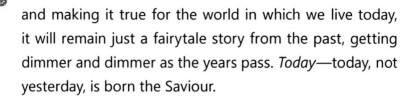

and making it true for the world in which we live today, it will remain just a fairytale story from the past, getting dimmer and dimmer as the years pass. *Today*—today, not yesterday, is born the Saviour.

Part One

THE CHRISTMAS STORY

John Henson

Chapter 1

SETTING THE SCENE

The Church down the ages has been playing the game of 'Chinese Whispers'. There is no better example of this than the Christmas stories as we portray them and celebrate them today. You will find the whispers passed on in most of the Christmas cards you are likely to receive at Christmas and in any Nativity plays in school or in church you find yourselves attending, willingly or otherwise. A careful look at the stories as they are told in the Gospels may alert you to the possibility that the Christmas card/ nativity scenes haven't got it quite right, or you may have been so entranced by the nativity play, or the familiarity of the Christmas cards may have given you such a warm Christmassy feeling, that you will actually read the Christmas stories through Christmassy eyes and see the innkeeper shaking his head to Mary and Joseph and showing them to the stable, and the shepherds bringing a lamb, followed by three kings on camels. You manage to do this, though none of those things is actually in the text. Sometimes the whispers get added to. There have now been nativity plays in which, to crown all, Father Christmas arrived at the stable, together with Rudolf the Red Nosed Reindeer. It could be argued that someone was making an interesting theological point. But it is more likely that the teachers in school had no respect for the true story, and goodness knows how confused the children were.

We may discuss at some length and not come to any conclusion as to what extent the Bible stories are literally true. I shall not be pressing you to take one line or another. Factual, or sort of poetry, the gospel writers tell the stories in order to convey a message. If we portray the story wrong, especially if we dress the story up in such a way that it becomes more like a pantomime, then we may also be conveying the wrong message, or no message at all. It is just 'pretty pretty'. I am not opposed to the nativity play. There are many attempts now, both in churches and on television to present a more realistic version, more like it really was, with some relevance to the needy and poor in the world today. Those of us who are Christians hardly ever stop bewailing the 'commercialization' of Christmas. But much of the blame lies at our own door if we preserve traditions and carols that produce a warm glow, but very little else to hang on to. Father Christmas will beat us every time. We should be in favour of joy, for it is an essential part of the Christmas message. But joy has to link to something more lasting than the creation of a warm atmosphere and fellow-feeling to help us through the winter months.

We are going to have another look at the stories we have heard so often, over and over again. I also want to tell you something about the particular approach I take to the scriptures. There are many different approaches that can be made to the Bible stories. The most difficult one is the literalist one. That's because first you must chose which translation you are going to be literalistic about. There are many good translations today, and they are all different. You are more likely to get at the truth by comparing, but you will still have to make choices about this or that. If you try the original Greek, scholars will tell you that there are now over 200 different manuscripts for you to choose from, with many variations, a variation or two for nearly every sentence. You do better to listen to the story, using your imagination. And you are better off listening to the story in your own language, the language of the twentieth first century, rather than the language of the sixteenth, seventeenth, eighteenth, nineteenth or even twentieth century.

Bishop John Shelby Spong, one of the bishops who gave advice with regard to Good As New, has his way of looking at the Christmas stories. He believes they are *midrash*. That is, they are stories based on the models of other stories, from the Hebrew scriptures or from other cultures of the ancient world. When people tell stories, they subconsciously model them on the basis of a story they have heard before. Witnesses giving testimonies in trials often arrange their story in the form they have heard in a trial on television or in a 'who done it'. That is not dishonest. It's what we all do when we tell somebody what we did on holiday. Jack Spong believes the Gospel writers were more aware of what they were doing than that. They deliberately used stories that would be familiar to people already, so that they would ring the bell of truth. Margaret Barker's book *Christmas, the Original Story* is a work of wide and thorough scholarship. She takes as her focus point the theology surrounding the Jewish Temple. At the time of Jesus, the temple was still the centre of Jewish worship. She reads the Christmas story in the light of Temple liturgies and the aspirations for a renewal of pure temple worship. I think she has gone too far in associating the whole of the Christmas story with temple theology. Although some friends and family of Jesus were associated with the temple, many other Jews of his day shared Jesus' disgust at the commercial aspects of the temple. John the Dipper, though of priestly stock, offered forgiveness and salvation outside and apart from the temple worship. A third line has been taken by Rowan Williams, who in a very frustrating debate with Richard Dawkins, said that the Christmas stories are best understood as poetry. Marcus Borg in his book *The First Christmas*, believes the stories are best understood as parables.

So what line do I take? Have you ever seen a 'Son et Lumière'? Usually it is a story told by means of coloured lights which, to the accompaniment of music or storytelling, are thrown on screens or the walls of buildings. When one light is shone, certain aspects of the buildings or receptive surface will stand out, but when another light is shown other aspects are revealed while the former ones fade. It is as if Jack Spong throws the light of *midrash* on the Christmas stories, and we see aspects of the stories and understand them better as a result of the light he sheds. The same with Margaret Barker's work. She too throws a different light on things. Jesus is the Messiah who fulfils many of the hopes and dreams of the religious of his day. However, the light I wish to show is somewhat different.

When I had completed my degree at Oxford I knew, and was told, that I had the choice of becoming an academic. For me it was never a choice. I wanted to be out in the world with ordinary people. I wanted to go home to Wales, and the valleys of Wales in particular, which were the centre of a distinctive working class culture. I had imbibed what I needed from centres of learning. I would continue to study and to learn. But I knew that Jesus was not primarily about relating to the priests and scholars of his day, though he was able to take them on. He was about relating to the fisher folk of Galilee, to the outcasts and the prostitutes. He spoke the Good News of God's New World in a way the common people could understand. I wanted to do the same. Jesus was interested in humanity; he was interested in individual people. That is my interest too. To what extent the stories are *midrash* or temple theology or poetry I don't know. They come across to me, like the rest of the Gospels, as stories about real people. Even if the facts are not strictly true, and even if the people did not actually exist, they are sufficiently well drawn by the writers that they come across as real people, like a realistic novel. I believe that is how the Gospel writers want us to understand them. As a historian, I have examined documents much less reliable and more contradictory than the Christian scriptures, yet historians have no difficulty in accepting them as evidence. They write their histories on the basis of them. I am interested in what sort of people Mary and Joseph were and what actually happened in Nazareth and Bethlehem in the first century. I am interested in how they and their situations relate to us. Unless there are some familiar experiences they and we share, I don't see much point in bothering with the stories at all.

Chapter 2

NAZARETH, NEXT STOP BETHLEHEM

When Lisa was six months pregnant, God sent Gabriel to Nazareth in the province of Galilee. Gabriel had a message for Mary, a young woman engaged to Joseph, a descendant of King David. Gabriel came into the house and said, 'Pleased to meet you, Mary. You're a special person. God thinks highly of you.' But Mary was nervous, trying to think what it was all about. So Gabriel said, 'Nothing to worry about, Mary. God is your friend. You're going to have a baby boy, and you're to call him Jesus. He will be famous and known as 'God's

Likeness'. God will make him the true successor of David, his ancestor. He'll have the permanent care of God's people, and they will go on increasing more and more.' Mary said, 'I don't see how that can be. I'm not married yet.' Gabriel said, 'God's Spirit has it all arranged. She will be responsible. 'God's Likeness' has to be very special. You'll also be pleased to know your cousin Lisa is pregnant. It's going to be a boy! Everyone had given up hope, but she's now six month's gone. There's no limit to what God can do! Mary said, 'Here I am

then, ready to help God all I can. May your words come true!'
Then God's agent left. (Luke 1:26 Good As New.)

Only two of our four Gospels attempt to relate the story of the birth of Jesus—Matthew and Luke. They are quite different from each other. Almost only two things are the same in both accounts. (1) Jesus was the son of a couple called Joseph and Mary. (2) The history of the birth revolves around two towns—Nazareth and Bethlehem. Even in this there is a significant difference.

Luke starts the story off in Nazareth and suggests that Nazareth was where Jesus' conception took place. Nazareth was in Galilee, in the north of the country. Galilee was semi-cosmopolitan, Jews living cheek by jowl with Gentiles. It was a long way from Jerusalem with its theological and ritual influence, strongly agricultural, with a peasant culture.

Matthew starts the story in Bethlehem. Bethlehem was in the more Jewish south, close to Jerusalem. It had a sense of history and destiny, for it was the birth town of David. It was a busy centre of government and trade, on the way to Egypt. It was sufficiently important to have at least one hotel or guest house, but Matthew does not mention any. The young Jesus is first located in a house in Bethlehem, and the impression given is that this was Joseph's house and that he and Mary had been there since the birth, possibly before. Not until the little family return from a period of asylum in Egypt is there any mention of

Nazareth, which they decide will be a safer place for them. There is therefore in Luke a movement from Nazareth to Bethlehem, whereas in Matthew the movement is from Bethlehem to Nazareth. Only by putting the two accounts together can we get the sort of story that comes out in our nativity plays. If you want to be theological you could say that in Luke a Galilean artisan family move to Bethlehem to establish an identity with David, whereas Matthew states from the beginning that Jesus' origin is in the town of David and that Jesus only moves to Nazareth as a place of refuge. Some scholars who come down very heavily on the side that the Gospel writers are simply doing theology, say that Nazareth was the probable birth place of Jesus and that Matthew and Luke simply invent different stories to link Jesus with Bethlehem.

For me, however, both Nazareth and Bethlehem seem very likely to have featured in the true historical event, but for very different reasons than the need to establish Jesus' Davidic credentials. Jesus himself, on an occasion when he was baiting the fundamentalist Pharisees, poured scorn on their literalist approach to scripture by tying them up in knots.

Jesus went on teaching in the temple. He said, 'I'm surprised the experts say God's Chosen One is to be a descendant of David, since David was inspired by God's Spirit to say,

God said to my Leader: 'Sit by me.
Then you'll have no enemy.'

If David calls the Chosen One his Leader, how can he be David's descendant?' This brought some chuckles from the crowd. (Mark 12:35 GAN)

Jesus was doing more than making fun of the Pharisees' literalist way of reading scripture. He was rubbishing the idea that it was necessary for the Messiah to be descended from David. This would mean, by implication, that whether Jesus was born in Bethlehem or not was irrelevant. Jesus was the person he was because he was the person he was, not because of either family or place of birth. If his parents did make a fuss out of the fact that Jesus had been born in Bethlehem, it made no odds to him. Maybe the real reason for the journey from Nazareth to Bethlehem and back again was a human one.

Nazareth was a little town up in the hills. It was regarded as not a good place to come from. Nathan (Nathanael), one of Jesus' friends, said when he first heard that Jesus came from Nazareth, *'Nazareth!? . . . Can anything good come from that dump?' (*Good As New pg.84) Compared with the Galileans who lived on the lake side and were in contact with Greek culture day by day, the people of Nazareth were uncouth. They were also intolerant. They hustled Jesus out of the Synagogue and very nearly did away with him, all because he talked about God's love for non-Jews. This was a place where the gossips would kill you, if nothing else did.

According to Catholic tradition, Mary was about thirteen when she conceived. It was not unusual to be married in your early teens in that society. Twelve was the official age of adulthood. But Mary was not married, only engaged. You could not expect the women of Nazareth to accept a cock and bull story of a virgin birth and it must be doubtful whether Mary or Joseph so much as thought about trying it. Nazareth was not the place for an unmarried mother. She would be outcast, probably stoned to death.

Luke includes in his birth story the visit of 'the angel' Gabriel to Mary and a subsequent holiday Mary had with her cousin Lisa (Elizabeth), in the hill country down south. Most of the angels in the Bible are human beings bringing help or a message from God. The nativity story as portrayed on UK television at Christmas 2010, got this right. The word 'angel' means a messenger. John the Dipper was an angel. What we should imagine is a sympathetic neighbour with suspicions. She or he has a quiet word with Mary, warning her what to expect perhaps. It was the message that frightened Mary, not the messenger. She calmed Mary by telling her that such unfortunate births could turn out to be in the will of God. After all, the great king Solomon had been born because David had a naughty relationship with

Bathsheba.

Mary packed her bag and went down south to visit her cousin. Lisa and Kerry lived up in the hills, not far from Jerusalem. As soon as Mary got there she greeted Lisa with a hug and a kiss. This made Lisa's baby jump inside her. It was God's Spirit, bringing the baby to life. Lisa spoke out loud, 'What a lucky woman you are, Mary. Your baby's going to be a wonderful person. I'm very honoured to have a visit from the mother of the one who's going to be my Leader. Your greeting got my baby moving. He must be pleased! It's always a good thing to believe what God tells us is going to happen.'

Then Mary sang this song for Lisa: (The Magnificat)
(Luke 1: 39-46 GAN)

The visit of Mary to Lisa seems very much like the visit of a young woman 'in distress' to a compassionate relative. Lisa was more the age of an aunt than a cousin. She herself had been the butt of scorn and isolation because she had been childless and would be likely to be sympathetic to Mary's plight. The Magnificat, though a song for Lisa, included Mary, for it was about those who were put to shame becoming famous. Possibly Lisa might be able to arrange something to help Mary in her shame? If Mary were to come back down south closer to the time of the likely birth, Lisa and her family might shield her. They were a priestly family and well connected. Anywhere was better than Nazareth! Less than a hundred years ago this was a very common story in our own land. Young women often had to go and stay for a few weeks with an aunt.

Augustus, the Roman Emperor, sent out an order for a census to be made of the population within the empire. The Governor of Syria, was responsible for managing the count in Palestine. Everybody went to their home town to have their names recorded. This meant that Joseph had to travel from Nazareth in the north to Bethlehem in the south. Bethlehem was the recognized home of all those descended from David. He took Mary, his partner, with him. She was pregnant. While they were in Bethlehem Mary went into labour and gave birth to her first child, a boy. Because there was no welcome for them in the hotel, they were living rough in the street. Mary dressed him in his baby clothes and put him in a feeding trough. (GAN pg 184 para 1)

The destination of the second journey down south, this time with Joseph, was also probably intended to be the home of Kerry and Lisa. But the couple did not make it. The baby was born en route at Bethlehem. The journey, probably on foot, with the possible lift for part of the way in an ox cart, would have been enough to bring about a premature birth. No mention of a donkey in the text. Nor is there a mention of a stable, or a cave—the two competing traditions about where Jesus was born (the stable 'western' and the cave 'eastern'). Jesus was put in a feeding trough. The feeding troughs would have been out on the street. The animals were tethered, like the Palm Sunday donkey, outside the houses. The baby was born out-of-doors. Imagine the scene! Women rushing from their houses, making a circle around the poor girl; others bringing water and towels, and strips of linen cloth, and doing what was necessary for her. (Swaddling bands indicate poverty. A wealthy person would have a seamstress to make baby clothes for a child. Poorer people just tore strips off their own clothes and wrapped the baby around.) Perhaps some kind of makeshift tent would have been made and the baby placed in the most convenient place, the nearest feeding trough. Difficult to make this into a nativity play. Perhaps it's not for children.

There is no way of getting away from the conclusion that Luke's telling of the story represents in part a 'cover-up.' He tells us that Mary and Joseph went to Bethlehem because of a census. Historians are now quite clear that no such census took place at this time, and that in any case it was not the custom for people to return to the town of their birth. Such a procedure would have caused chaos and been much resented. Whether the cover-up was Luke's idea or that of his informant, there is no means of telling. Someone was anxious to provide a smidgeon of dignity to a story where very little dignity existed. That is, not dignity as usually understood. There is a human dignity to the story, which shines above the low gossip of the inhabitants of Nazareth and the selfishness and lack of human sympathy of those in charge of the accommodation in Bethlehem. As soon as we get over the shock of the story-teller's cover up, the whole matter of the 'Inn' and the 'Innkeeper' takes on a different aspect. It is now no longer 'there was no room in the inn' because of the number of visitors to Bethlehem for the census'. Without the fictional census the local establishments would more than likely have enough places to accommodate the usual run of visitors and traders with the odd room to spare. 'No room in the inn' meant 'no welcome in the inn'. It was like the large table of the Mad Hatter and the March Hare in *Alice in Wonderland*. The table was set for many people, but when Alice arrived, the Hatter and the Hare cried, 'No room, no room!' Alice remarked contemptuously, 'There's plenty of room!' In the 1950s the black man from the West Indies could try street after street in London, filled with guest houses sporting 'vacancies', until he knocked at the door, when the vacancies card was turned around the other way.

There was no room anywhere in Bethlehem except out on the street for the obviously pregnant teenage girl who should have been at home with her mother, nor for the inexperienced teenage lad with her. Women were strictly confined during pregnancy in that culture. They certainly did not go wandering the streets, unless they were prostitutes. Women were unclean during the process of birth and would continue so after the birth until they made a visit to the temple for ritual cleansing. A hotel was no place for births, especially not irregular ones. The hotel would be affected by the uncleanness and the shedding of blood. Respectable guests would be outraged.

I remember the days when a large hotel in the middle of Cardiff refused to house a gay conference. They changed their minds when the Trade Union Congress threatened to put them on their list of banned hotels. There was no TUC to come to the aid of Mary and Joseph. The true scenario also makes less likely the provision of accommodation in a canopied stable in the hotel courtyard, or even a nearby stable housed in a cave. And here we must commend Luke. He tells this part of the story as it was. Whatever the reason for there being no room in the inn, Jesus and his parents are refused accommodation, and no adequate alternative accommodation of even the lowest quality is suggested or described by Luke. The theme of Jesus' rejection by his own people, which Luke will develop later in his gospel, is introduced by the unadorned picture of his rejection in Bethlehem.

This is how Jesus, God's Chosen, was born. His mother Mary was engaged to Joseph. She was pregnant before they were married. This was the work of God's Spirit. Joseph, her fiancé, was a good man. He did not want to expose Mary to a public scandal, so he thought to break off the engagement without making any fuss. When he had almost made up his mind to do this, he had a message from God in a dream.

'Joseph, remember you're a descendant of David. There's no need to have any worries about marrying Mary. This baby has been planned by God's Spirit. It's going to be a boy and

you must call him Jesus. He will be a healer and cure people of their wrongdoing.'

The birth of Jesus reminds us of words spoken by one of God's speakers in times past 'A young woman will become pregnant and give birth to a son. He will be the sign that God is with us.'

When Joseph woke up, he took God's advice and got married to Mary. They did without sex until the baby boy was born. Joseph called him Jesus. (Matthew 1:18-end)

And what about Joseph? Matthew tells his story. The author is an old fashioned sort of Jew, and looks at things from the man's point of view. In contrast to Luke, women's champion, Matthew hardly mentions Mary. Joseph is a man who does the decent thing. We don't know his age. My gut feeling is that he was not much older than Mary, perhaps in his middle teens. We do not know whether or not he was the human father. What we do know is that the neighbours talked. There is evidence elsewhere in the gospels that the whiff of scandal followed the family ever after. Some of Jesus' enemies accused him of being a Samaritan (John 8:48—Good As New pg 99). When the religious authorities were questioning the man Jesus had given sight to, they said of Jesus, 'As for this fellow, we don't even know his racial background' (John 9:29 GAN) There is an old tradition dating from very early on in the Christian church (mid 100s *Barker pg 132)* that Jesus had been sired by a Roman soldier called Panthera. This was the view of some Christians. Maybe some Roman Christians wanted to feel that Jesus was one of them? Rape of local girls by occupying military has always been common. But one thing is clear. Both Matthew and Luke believed Joseph to be the father. Both of them trace Jesus' descent from David through Joseph, not through Mary. (Matthew 1 & Luke 3:23) Twice in Luke's telling of the encounter between Mary and Gabriel he emphasises the relationship of Jesus as a descendent of David through Joseph 'Gabriel had a message for Mary, a young woman engaged to Joseph, a descendent of King David'. And Gabriel says of Jesus, 'God will make him the true successor of David, his ancestor.' (2:26-) And we must not forget that Luke sets a scenario about a census in which he makes clear that it is Joseph who was obliged as a descendent of David to make the journey to Bethlehem, because Bethlehem was the family home of the Davidic clan. It was Joseph who was to certify Jesus' descent from David. It was Joseph who carried David's seed, or as we would say today David's genes. The phrase in Luke *as was supposed* (3:23 KJV) is a very obvious addition from a later commentator. It makes a nonsense of Luke's painstaking exercise of tracing Jesus back to David through Joseph. If we want to keep the addition, a good in-context translation would be 'as the neighbours knew full well'. Both Matthew and Luke wish to convince their Jewish readers that Jesus was Messiah. In order to be so, according to Jewish thinking, Jesus had to descend from David and from David's father Jesse. To assert otherwise, or even to hint at an irregularity would be as much as saying that Jesus was not Messiah. Luke has Paul saying in Acts (2 Luke) 13: 22 *'This is what God said about David.' David, Jesse's son, is the sort of person I like . . . . 'God has given us a descendent of David to be our Healer, as promised'* (Acts 13:22 GAN). If they had wanted to argue for a virgin birth in our narrow understanding of the word 'virgin', Matthew and Luke would have had to trace Jesus' ancestry through Mary. It would not have been beyond their powers to do so. Both trace Jesus back to David via Joseph in different ways, employing a certain amount of imaginative invention. But it was vitally important to the future of the Jewish strand of the Christian community that they made absolutely clear their belief that Joseph was Jesus' father. Fundamentalists and traditionalists like to pick and choose when it comes to the passages they wish to construct their immovable dogmas upon. We liberals also pick and choose, but we admit it. If you insist on a literal virgin birth on the grounds of inerrant scripture, then you must insist on Joseph's parentage on the grounds of inerrant scripture. Adoption is not an option. It would have been insufficient to convince Hebrew minds. Their Messiah had to be 100% kosher.

The 'Virgin Birth' cannot be substantiated on scriptural grounds. It is an interpretation stemming from later theology. It has got into the creeds, and some sections of the Church are stuck with it. The Greek for 'virgin' (parthenos) then more generally meant 'a woman of marriageable age', or 'a woman who has not yet given birth to a child', and so does the Hebrew equivalent, *and* the Latin 'virgo'. ('Virgo intacta' is the Latin for virgin in the narrow sense.) The words in Matthew "do not fear to take Mary as your wife etc." (1:20) to some seem evidence that Joseph did not think himself the father. In first century Jewish eyes, whoever the father, whether Joseph or someone else, Mary, by putting herself in a position to become pregnant before marriage, would be marked down as a wanton woman, a seducer, a whore—fit to be Joseph's mistress perhaps, but unworthy of being his wife. The same was true in the sixteenth century. Anne Boleyn, unlike her sister Mary Boleyn, refused to have sex with Henry VIII until they were married. Otherwise, like her sister, she would have made herself unworthy of the King and unworthy to be Queen. Difficult for us to understand nowadays when engaged couples or even those who have only just begun courting, are expected to have sex. The words about Mary and Joseph not having sex until the baby is born may simply mean, as in Good As New, that they did without sex during that time. The implications of the angel's message is that Mary was already expecting at this point and that Joseph knew it. Certainly the suggestion is that after the birth sexual relations would resume. There are no grounds here for Mary being a perpetual virgin

Both Luke and Matthew say that the birth will be the work of God's Spirit. (Luke 1:35/ Matthew 1:20) So was John the Dipper, so was Adam, so was every other human being. . .

(Luke 1:14 of John 'He shall be filled with the Holy Spirit from his mother's womb' and 1:41 'When Elizabeth heard Mary's greeting, the child leapt in her womb. And Eiilizabeth was filled with the Holy Spirit.')

Much depends on the interpretation and translation of the Greek text. It is possible with honesty to read a virgin birth both in Matthew and Luke's account, and probably this option will be taken until the end of time. But in that case honesty also dictates an admission that there is inconsistency in the texts, with a competing assertion that Joseph is the genuine human father. Some people take as an *a priori* that the scriptures cannot be inconsistent, but that is their problem!

The 'Virgin Birth' is a very unfortunate by-product of the Gnostic heresy in which the flesh was regarded as evil. Most evil of all was sexual contact, so Jesus could not have been born by that means. Forever, it would seem, Christians have to live with the idea in the back of their consciousness that sex is impure. Today we are looking ever more ridiculous with all our sexual hang-ups. If God could use a woman's womb to become incarnate, why not a man's testicles and penis? If the idea horrifies you, I rest my case! I'm not telling anyone they must not believe in the Virgin Birth, and I am not claiming an alternative infallibility to that of the Pope. But surely this is not the way God goes about things? Every baby born is miraculous. The 'Virgin Birth' down-grades the birth of other babies, and God would not want that.

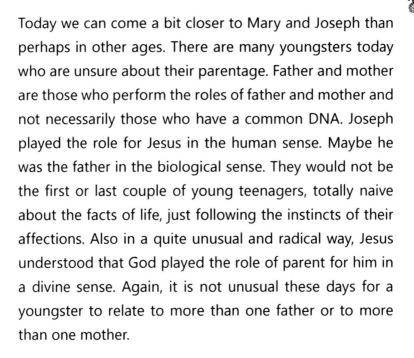

Today we can come a bit closer to Mary and Joseph than perhaps in other ages. There are many youngsters today who are unsure about their parentage. Father and mother are those who perform the roles of father and mother and not necessarily those who have a common DNA. Joseph played the role for Jesus in the human sense. Maybe he was the father in the biological sense. They would not be the first or last couple of young teenagers, totally naive about the facts of life, just following the instincts of their affections. Also in a quite unusual and radical way, Jesus understood that God played the role of parent for him in a divine sense. Again, it is not unusual these days for a youngster to relate to more than one father or to more than one mother.

You might think that if Joseph were the human father, he would also have been under condemnation from the Nazareth mob. Not necessarily so. It was the woman who got the blame in those days, just like Eve. Remember the story of the woman caught in adultery and brought to Jesus for judgement? They didn't bring the man! It would have been said that the slut Mary had seduced a pure, young, innocent boy. That's the way people thought in those days. It was a man's world. All the same, we get the impression that Joseph loved Mary and resolved boldly to stand by her.

Two Star-Struck Lovers

Two star-struck lovers
Following their senses;
No one warned them
About the consequences.

Then come the holy ones,
Uptight to their eyes,
Teach that sex is dirty,
Feed us porky pies.

Divine we see embodied
For ever and a day;
But we are not allowed to think
God came the usual way. (John Henson)

God's Messenger to Mary Came

God's messenger to Mary came one day,
He said, 'My name is Gabriel, okay?'
'I have surprising news for you–
I've called to say
You're going to have a baby–
Hooray, hooray, hooray!'

Some will cry 'shame' and turn their backs on you,
But you will gather friends both kind and true.
His origin's a mystery, but just for now;

A child for everybody!
That's the why and how!

Then Mary lost her fears and she replied,
'Whatever God thinks best I'm on God's side.
I'll sing a song of liberty and face the day.
I'm going to have a baby-
Hooray, hooray, hooray!'

Then Joseph did the decent thing—stood by;
'I'm going to be a Dad, so there, don't cry!
We'll travel down to Bethlehem,
There'll be less fuss.
Though many will be hostile,
This means 'God with us!'

So in the street outside the Inn Love came,
God's joy and peace to us in human frame;
And we can join the curious few who came to say,
'He is our little wonder!
Hooray, hooray, hooray!'

(After Sabine Baring-Gould 1834-1924)

REHABILITATING MARY, MOTHER OF JESUS, TO FULL SEXUALITY.

It is to be hoped that Mary can look forward to a better deal in the twenty first century than she has had from the last two centuries. She has been confined to a half life, both pietistic and sloppy, robbing her of her true flesh and blood. Being fully sexual requires not only the birthing of a child but experiencing the real biological and emotional process that results in the conception of a child, like every other human being. Being a mother requires for most, not only the recollection of the trauma and pain, followed (not always) by a sense of triumph, but if not by triumph, by exhaustion and a special type of relaxation. It requires the carnal knowledge that brought you to that place. Sexual intercourse can be messy, not quite as bad as birth, but fleshly and bloody none the less. It is an important experience. It is also divine, symbolizing of the union between earth and heaven maybe, but also having quality in its own right. A mother needs this background. So does the father. So do both of them together, whatever be their history or their likely future. We also have a de-masculated and prematurely aged Joseph. He must be this to protect Mary from the corrupting experience of sex. For Mary the Virgin's message is that sex is at best a necessary evil, made unecessary in her case. At worst sex is a great big evil responsible for the sin of the whole human race—to be avoided if you can. Only when Mary is rehabilitated will she be able to teach us that sex is a glorious gift from God, one of God's best, not just for having little babies, but for sharing affection with others, and for enjoying in all its mulitfarious aspects and varieties. The same is true for Joseph. Whether or not he is the true father, he is not impotent. Because his sexuality is in full working order he can get into the fatherly role, and also continue to increase the family with Mary. When we have a rehabilitated Mary and Joseph, then we will have a Holy Family we can relate to, whatever our sexuality. Because the experience of sexuality is something we all have, whatever its variety, and its wholeness in its practice we all can celebrate.

The Virgin Birth and the 'Droit de Seigneur'.

The Medieval doctrine of the Virgin Birth looks scarily like an interpretation of scripture that sees the Lord of the Domaine exercising his unquestionable right ('Droit de Seigneur'*) as owner of body, mind and soul of all his underlings, to push aside the husband or betrothed of his female servant and impregnate her himself. It would be as bad to the more civilized sensitivities of the twenty-first century as the idea, also Medieval, that God the Father's paternal rights include nominating his dutiful son as the whipping boy for others' misdomeaners. When are we going to chuck the theology of the Middle Ages?

---

*   (Despite the popularization of Beaumarchais' political satire 'The Marriage of Figaro' by Mozart, the 'Droit de Seigneur' was still exercised well into the twentieth century, and there may still be cases of it today. See the film 'Gosford Park'.)

Chapter 3

MINSTRELS AND MAGICIANS

Some Were Warm

Some were warm and some were not
When, all snug in feeding trough,
Smiled with wind a baby brown,
Jesus, born in David's Town.
Chorus:
Welcome, very special day;
All our cares seem less some way;
Sing from Neath* to Kazakhstan,
God is found in Bethlehem.

'Say, you smelly shepherds low,
Why are you excited so?
Why have you left sheep and lamb
In the fields, exposed to harm?
Chorus . . .

---

*   Or 'Sing from Maine, Slough, Stoke, Cork, Mull, Devon to . . . etc.'

'As we watched at dead of night,
Wandering minstrels caused us fright;
But they brought Good News in song,
Told us we should haste along.'
Chorus . . . .

Two years later sorcerers came,
With a message much the same;
They looked quite peculiar,
Had been following a star!
Chorus . . . .

Weird and unwashed join to praise,
On this merriest of days,
One who came for people all,
Not just the respectable.
Chorus . . . .

(After Edward Caswell 1814-78 'See amid the winter's snow'.)

That night, down in the fields nearby, some sheep farmers were guarding their sheep. One of God's agents approached them. There was a strange light, which frightened the farmers. The agent said, 'Don't panic. I've some good news for everybody. A baby has just been born in Bethlehem. He's going to be our new Leader, God's Chosen, the one we've been waiting for. If you want to see him, he's in a feeding

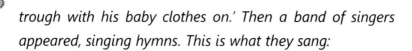

trough with his baby clothes on.' Then a band of singers appeared, singing hymns. This is what they sang:

**'Look at God's beauty around and above,
We bring you God's peace and a bundle of love.'**

When the songsters had faded into the distance, the sheep farmers said, 'Why don't we go up to Bethlehem and find out what it's all about? God's been speaking to us.' So they ran as fast as they could, and found the baby in the feeding trough being cared for by Mary and Joseph. Then the farmers told everybody what they had learnt about the baby. Their story was hard to believe. But Mary remembered their words and thought deeply about them. The sheep farmers went back to the fields, singing songs to God as they went. They had seen and heard such wonderful things.(Luke 2:8 GAN)

When I was a child I found it very difficult to distinguish between angels and fairies. You could either have a fairy or an angel at the top of your Christmas tree. In either case it was a doll in the shape of a very artificial looking android with wings. Where did we get our images of the Christmas angels from? When you think of the heavenly choir that sang in the fields below the town of Bethlehem, what comes into your mind? The Christmas card image is probably very well stamped on your subconscious. You may be keen on the apocalyptic books of the Bible—Daniel, Ezekiel, Revelation—where angels can fly about, though there is not often a mention of wings. They didn't need them. Wings appeared on angels somewhere in the Middle Ages. Forget the seraphim of Isaiah. They were flying serpents attending God's throne. The cherubim were winged bulls, like those of the Babylonians. They pulled God's chariot. Or we may be influenced by the tradition of robed choirs. All those highly washed and clean choir boys singing 'Once in royal . . . .' Just stick a pair of wings on and you've got your angel.

If Margaret Barker is right, the heavenly choir were on loan from the Temple. For her everything is temple. If the shepherds had a vision, the temple and its multitude of candles and swirling incense would provide the backdrop.

But the shepherds lived their lives out in the fields. They never got to the temple or the synagogue. Working hours would not allow it. This meant they were numbered among the outcasts, the unwashed and despised. Contact with animals, dead animals very often, rendered them permanently unclean. Where would they get their music? They would make it themselves, with a five-stringed harp like David, and something like the pipes of Pan. And they would sing. With no noise of traffic or the shouting of the streets, the acoustics would be perfect. Sometimes it must have really taken off and they would experience a high. The songs they sang? Dreary old temple chants? Not on your life. There were pop songs in those days, though now long forgotten. There were little troupes of singers who would tour the inns and market places, accompanied by pipe and drum. And they would dance as well. Jesus saw them and liked them. It made him want to dance. He was 'Lord of the dance'.

Did one of these groups of minstrels pass by that night, singing as they came? Their voices to begin with waft in the distance, getting louder and louder, but never too loud, never deafening. We would find their music strange. It wouldn't be Handel's Messiah, or any of our Christmas carols. Different scales, and different intervals between the notes from what we are used to, and very strange rhythms. I think they must have been coming down the hill from Bethlehem, for they brought the news of the baby born in the street. It was a very public birth. Almost everyone would have got to see the baby, or got to know about it. The warm hearted would have rejoiced and offered a bit of tender loving care towards the family. This was an event not to be missed. Someone had organized a birthday party. Better get up the hill to Bethlehem quickly. God has done it again, worked another miracle. Mother and child are doing fine!

Angels sing. There is a heavenly song of praise that continues down the ages. But it is not confined to cathedrals or charismatic worship songs. Perhaps we catch more of the spirit of it when, as frequently in Cardiff, we see a band of Hare Krishna people, singing and dancing down the street. We hear it in popular Christmas songs such as 'Mary's boy child' and 'See him lying on a bed of straw', but also in 'the Manic Street Preachers' and many another twenty first century pop group where the words, if you can catch them, are full of message. At the first Christmas they sang a rhyme that went something like,

> **'Look at God's beauty around and above,**
> **We bring you God's peace and a bundle of love'**

Jesus was born in Bethlehem during the reign of Herod the Great. Some magicians from Persia travelled to Jerusalem. They asked, 'Where's the new baby who will lead God's people when he grows up? We've seen a new star which tells us he's been born. We want to pay our respects to him.' This news put Herod into a state of panic which frightened the people of Jerusalem. Herod called together the religious leaders and experts in the old books and asked them where God's Chosen was likely to be born. They turned his attention to Bethlehem, quoting words from one of God's speakers:

> **'Bethlehem, there's no reason for you to think you are not important.**
> **You are going to be the birthplace of someone who will lead my people like a shepherd'**

Herod had a private meeting with the magicians, and found out from them the precise time the star appeared. Then he gave them directions for Bethlehem and said, 'Do your best to find the little boy. I would like to pay him my respects too.'

When they had heard what Herod had to say, they continued their journey. They spotted the new star again. It seemed to move on in front of them and stop over the house where the boy lived. They got very excited by this. They went inside the house and met Jesus and his mother and expressed their pleasure at the honour they felt. They took out from their luggage the presents they had brought with them including money, medicine and perfume. They had a hunch it would be a mistake to go back to Herod, so they took a different route back home. (Matthew 2: 1-12)

I have given up sending Christmas cards, with the exception of my old school teacher, Miss Dobson, in Tiverton, now in her eighties. I tell my friends not to send them to me. Some do, just to annoy me. And if they want to annoy me further, they send me a card with three kings on camels. Margaret Barker does a good job here, tracing the origins of the three kings legend. The Magi, as the word suggests, means 'magicians'. They were a Persian order, Zoroastrians, and a king could join, though he would be most unlikely to get the time off to go and see Herod. If he did, it would have been a much trumpeted international event, and Herod would not have contemplated assassinating another head of state. The number is unspecified, and in the earliest Christian paintings in Rome there were two, three or four. Before the legends of the kings developed, there was a legend among the Greeks dating from around 200 C.E. that they were Greek philosophers. Matthew's use of the Magi was possibly to let Zoroastrians know they were welcome to become members of God's Bright New World. Like the Jews, they were monotheists. Like the Jews they looked forward to the coming of a saviour figure, 'the Sashoyant', though for Zoroastrians he would not be the saviour in a narrow nationalist sense, but a 'bringer of good' for the whole world.

This may give us the hint as to why legends, or Chinese whispers, develop. A group understands the story as being the story for them. The Magi turned into kings in the Middle Ages when monarchies in Europe were struggling to establish themselves, especially against the powers of the Church, as in England where Henry II and Thomas Becket crossed swords. 'The Three Kings' was a way of advertising. 'What do you need? You need a king, just like the lovely kings who came to see the baby Jesus.' Royal propaganda! Possibly still is. Some Christian asylum seekers from Pakistan told my daughter they were surprised to see the Magi dressed up as kings, because back at home they were dressed as wizards. That's because the Greek was translated correctly into the Urdu as 'wizards'. 'Kings' gets everything wrong. Kings are respectable, or they and their followers think they are. The Magi were anything but respectable from a Jewish point of view. Zoroastrianism had been debased by the introduction of occult practices, such as star-gazing and consulting the dead. The Jewish writer of Matthew knew that wizards were forbidden by the Jewish law. Apart from anything else, they were Gentiles. There were probably women among them. Soothsayers were often female. The men would probably have some concubines with them, even their wives perhaps. These people were spooky and weird. We would no more honour them in church today than we would invite Russell Grant or Mystic Meg to preach the sermon. They were New Age people, spiritual freaks or geeks.

The single of Magi is Magus, as in 'Simon Magus', Simon the Magician in Acts 8—someone who has suffered from a bad press. He was a Christian convert. The word could also be the origin of the name MAGdalene attached to Mary, one of Jesus' inner circle of friends. In Good As New we call her 'Maggie', which sounds like the female of 'magus'. She was thought to have been infested by devils before she met Jesus. Maybe she was a witch, good with the potions and spells and fortune-telling. Paul also added a fortune-teller to his team at Philiptown.

Matthew, no less than Luke, is saying right from the start of the Gospel that it was outsiders who welcomed Jesus, not the religious or respectable or royalty. In Matthew's genealogy of Jesus there are five women, if you include Mary his mother. Five is a Jewish holy number, since there are five books of Moses. Every one of these women is sexually naughty. Look them up. Tamar, Rahab, Ruth, Bathsheba. Matthew portrays Mary as being no exception. Yet they represent God's love line. They carry the genes that are to appear in God's Chosen Messiah. Jesus said, *'I came not to call the righteous, but outcasts.'* Let's bring back the magicians, and let's bring back the true magic into our Christmas.

I am grateful to my friend Peterson Toscano for drawing attention to the fact that when the magicians visited Jesus in the Bethlehem home, they met only the toddler Jesus and his mother Mary. In his dramatic presentation entitled 'Jesus has two daddies' Peterson speculates what Joseph's reactions might have been when he arrived home to learn that Mary had been visited by a group of strange men, who left behind some generous gifts. The absence of Joseph may seem strange to us, until we remember that in those days it was the responsibility of the mother to look after young children and that fathers did not get paternity leave. A working man would spend very little time at home, and Joseph's work as a carpenter or mason, possibly in the Temple at Jerusalem, could keep him away from home for days. He looks to have been sleeping on his own when he had his dream telling him to take his family to Egypt. As we have seen, the Magi may have included men and women. There is no need to conclude that it caused strains in the couple's relationship. But I like Peterson's imaginative and human approach to scripture that sometimes takes us to edges and into corners we rarely visit.

As With Gladness Travellers Bold

As with gladness travellers bold
Saw a new star, pure as gold,
As with joy they caught its light,
Leading onward, beaming bright;
So, dear loving God may we,
On life's quest, your splendour see.

In our minds we see them come,
Jesus, to your lowly home;
There we watch them kneel before
You, the one the true adore;
So may we find such a place
Where we glimpse your smiling face.

As they offered gifts most rare
At your lodging poor and bare,
So may we with holy glee,
Freed from pride and vanity,
All we value gladly bring
For your use, our friend and king.

Loving Jesus, every day
Keep us in your joyful way;
When our time on earth is past,
Bring us travellers still, at last,
Where we need no star to guide,
Where no clouds your beauty hide.

In that heavenly country bright
We will need no other light;
You its light, its joy, its crown,
You the sun that goes not down.
There forever, gone all tears,
We will worship with the Seers.

(After W.C. Dix 1837-98)

When the magicians had gone, someone sent by God came to Joseph during the night with the message, 'You had better get your wife and little boy out of Bethlehem right away. Egypt would be the best place to make for. Don't come back until I get word to you that it's safe. Herod is sending out a search party. He's bent on murder! ' So Joseph that very night fled with his family and sought asylum in Egypt. They lived there until Herod's death. This calls to mind God's words in the old books,

'I brought my people out of Egypt.'

When Herod realised the magicians had given him the slip, he went berserk. He sent his soldiers to Bethlehem and the villages nearby to kill all the children who were two years old or less. He used the information he had from the magicians to work out about how old the child would be. The people of Bethlehem experienced what Jeremy had spoken about in years gone by.

'In ancient Ram a noise is heard,
Wailing, loud and wild;
Rachel has lost her little ones
And will not be consoled.'

After Herod had died, Joseph had another message from God. 'It's safe now for you to go back to your own land. Those who wanted to kill your little boy have died.' So Joseph took his family back to Palestine. But when he found out that Herod's son (Archie) had succeeded his father as ruler in the south of the country, Joseph was afraid to go back to Bethlehem. He was guided instead to Galilee in the north. The family set up home in the town of Nazareth. That's why Jesus is sometimes called 'The Nazarene'. (Matthew 2:13-23 GAN)

Joseph's Dreams

Names were important at the time of Jesus. They were meant to connect the recipient to someone important in the past. Jesus was thus linked to Joshua (the same name). Jesus' father Joseph was linked to Joseph, the favourite son of Jacob. So when Matthew tells the story of the second Joseph, he portrays him as a dreamer, like the first Joseph, so the reader would subconsciously make the link, 'O yes, that's right, of course.' Joseph's angels may have been human. He may have had a friend in Bethlehem, his prospective 'best man' perhaps, who had a chat with him late at night. Or it may have been one of the local rabbis, a progressive rabbi who counselled him to put the needs of the one he loved before the letter of the law. But it is just as likely that the 'angel' was within Joseph himself. Night-time was the time when he reflected and sorted himself out, when his conscience worked overtime. Bedtime for me is usually a good sleep. But sometimes it is for wrestling with a problem, even with writing a sermon. Come the morning it is all sorted out. This happened to Joseph three times in the story.

A week later the time came to give the baby boy his name and to remove his foreskin. He was called Jesus, as God's agent had suggested before he was conceived.

There were special ceremonies going back to the time of Moses, which Mary and Joseph went to Jerusalem for. Jesus had to be given as a present to God. (The old books say, 'The first boy born in every family shall belong to God.') They also made the customary gift to God of two pigeons.

Simeon lived in Jerusalem. He was a good man and carried out the duties of his religion. He was looking forward to better days for his country. God's Spirit was with him, and she told him he wouldn't die before seeing God's Chosen. She led him to the worship centre at the same time as Mary and Joseph were bringing in the baby Jesus. Simeon took Jesus in his arms and sang this song of thanks to God.

Your helper, God, moves on content,
Your plans my eyes have seen;
A new day dawns for every land,
Beyond your people's dream.

Joseph and Mary couldn't believe what Simeon had to say about Jesus. He gave the three of them his good wishes, and said to Mary, 'Your son will bring out the best and the worst in our people. He'll get into trouble for showing up so many in their true light. And you will share his pain.'

Anne was one of God's speakers. She came from a good family. She was eighty-four years of age, a widow whose husband had died just seven years after their marriage. She lived in the worship centre and did all she could to help, eating very little and talking with God on behalf of others, day and night. She came up to Mary and Joseph and said words of thanks to God for the baby. Then she introduced him to those who had their country's best interests at heart, as their hope for the future.

When Mary and Joseph had completed their business in Jerusalem, they went back home to Nazareth in Galilee. Jesus was a healthy baby, and grew up to be a strong and bright lad. People sensed there was something special about him. (Luke 2:21-39 GAN)

Simeon and Anne

This is the neglected part of the birth story. For Margaret Barker it is proof positive that the Temple is at the centre of the Christmas story. But in fact the remark that Mary and Joseph went to Jerusalem *'as the custom was'*, suggests that it was a matter of form rather than enthusiasm. It would have been a chore for a mother who had only given birth the week before. It would have been expensive too. They made you pay through the nose at the temple. Simeon was not the priest in charge of the ceremonies. He was an old man who hung around the place. Anne was also old and as a woman was not allowed into the inner part of the temple. Most cathedrals today have a few odd types perpetually hanging around them. They are part of the furniture. Anne was obliged to hear the daily prayer by the men thanking God that they were 'not a slave, nor a Gentile, nor a woman'. These two old people were non-conformists. They were there to see that people encountered a touch of humanity to offset the performance that went on up at the altar. Anne, like her namesake Hannah, was also childless, thus despised by the religious. Anne ate very little. We can believe that. She lived on the charity of those who came into the temple, already fleeced at the money changing tables and the gift stalls. Simeon and Anne were poor, needy people, victims of ageism, sexism in Anne's case, and the want of a social security system. They welcomed Jesus and gave him the extra attention and praise he would not have received from the priests who just went through the motions. Only Simeon and Anne in the temple spotted the baby who was the hope for the future.

Chapter 4

THE MISSING FIGURE
IN THE TABLEAU

My father was keen on nativity plays. He wrote many of them himself. They always had a modern theme. Modern, that is for the 1950s and 60s. They would be dated and a bit naff nowadays. Whatever the modern plot—someone who had lost their faith due to bereavement was one—we somehow managed to end up with shepherds, angels with wings, and three kings. I played the black one, face covered in boot polish. The final scene was a tableau with all the cast.

Included in the tableau would be Herod, the villain of the piece, standing behind the Magi, skulking and looking nasty. In a pantomime, the villain, Abanazar, the Rat King, the Wicked Fairy or whoever, usually comes down the steps with the other characters at the end, to boos instead of cheers. But they are still somehow alive and active. And we know that the pantomime story would have fallen flat without them. We are inclined to leave Herod out of the tableau these days. But he has an essential role to play.

Without him, and what he represents, the Christmas story would be incomplete.

Herod was known in his century and is still known today as Herod the Great. It says something about his historical importance. Very few rulers have been accorded that title. Alexander, Alfred, Charlemagne, Rhodri Fawr of Wales, Peter and Catherine of Russia. Why Herod? Partly the length of his reign, which was very unusual at the time. He reigned for fifty years. He reigned over most of what today we call the Holy Land and a bit more. He ruled in the name of Rome, but Rome trusted him, and within his own territories he was a vigorous and tyrannical ruler. But he got things done. He presided over a time of peace when there was no threat of invasion from without or insurrection within. That also was unusual. He put into position all the amenities that were associated with the Roman Empire— roads, bridges, aqueducts, baths, amphitheatres and so on. Most of all he built a magnificent new temple for the Jewish people. All these public works created jobs, brought in trade and boosted the economy. Lots of people profited from Herod's reign. His title was 'King of the Jews'. But he was only half Jewish, and in the eyes of enthusiasts for the Jewish faith, he was half-hearted in his zeal and observances. But in many respects he showed a care for his people. When there was a famine he sold the royal gold plate in order to provide food for the poor, and he relaxed the payment of debts.

Most dictators who live for a long time outlive their good works and become power obsessed. Power corrupts. Herod became intensely paranoid, always looking out for enemies, including among his own family. He killed two of his sons, a wife and a mother-in-law, and at the end when he was dying he ordered his courtiers to be killed to ensure mourning. There is no historical corroboration for the massacre of the children of Bethlehem, but such an action would have been completely within his character. When the magicians visited him and told him a new king had been born, Herod was put into a state of panic. Reason went out of the window. We are told that Herod's demeanour frightened the people of Jerusalem. So it might. They did not know what Herod might do. Might he take it out on the Jerusalem townsfolk? Craftily the experts in the old books directed the Magi to Bethlehem. If anyone was going to suffer, let it be the people down the road. Jerusalem was the city of David; it had been his capital. But so was Bethlehem, because that was where David had been born. If it was someone of the House of David the Magi had in mind, better it was one of the Bethlehem folk. There were plenty of people who claimed descent from David in Bethlehem as in Jerusalem, so why have the massacre here?

If we were writing a nativity play today, and wanted it to be up-to-date, who would we put in the tableau at the back, behind the magicians? Would it be one of the world's current clutch of ruthless dictators? Or would it be a

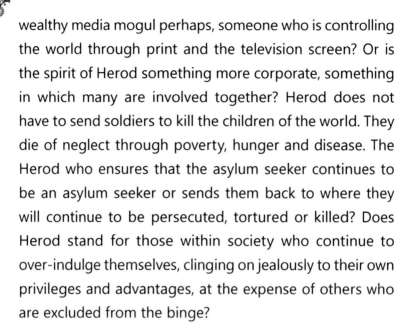

wealthy media mogul perhaps, someone who is controlling the world through print and the television screen? Or is the spirit of Herod something more corporate, something in which many are involved together? Herod does not have to send soldiers to kill the children of the world. They die of neglect through poverty, hunger and disease. The Herod who ensures that the asylum seeker continues to be an asylum seeker or sends them back to where they will continue to be persecuted, tortured or killed? Does Herod stand for those within society who continue to over-indulge themselves, clinging on jealously to their own privileges and advantages, at the expense of others who are excluded from the binge?

The challenge for Christians is to avoid being an incognito Herod. Herod was great, and there are a lot of ancient ruins to bear witness to his greatness. Love came down at Christmas in the form of a little baby who belonged to a family in distress. The Christmas story is about the competing claims of Herod and Jesus on every one of us. Christmas is about facing up to which of the two we wish to be identified with.

Chapter 5

THE DIVINE PERSPECTIVE

In the beginning God spoke. This is just like God—part of the way God is. Everything there is comes from God speaking; otherwise there would be nothing at all. God speaking brought into being the life and intelligence we all share. These have kept on shining like light in the darkness and have never been defeated by the darkness. There was a messenger from God called John. John played his part in keeping the light shining, encouraging people to trust the light, although he was not the light himself. The full light that makes things clear to everybody was then coming into the world. The one who made the world appeared in the world, but the world paid no attention. Those specially prepared, God's chosen people, turned their backs. Nevertheless there were many who opened their arms in trust, and these are the rightful children of God. They are not children in the human sense, the result of family planning or physical passion, but in the sense of sharing God's nature. God spoke by means of a human being who shared a tent on our campsite. We have seen the beauty of the only complete physical expression of The Loving God, wonderful to look at and to know. John showed his support by shouting out, 'This is the one I was telling you about, 'The one who arrives after me is more important than me, because he existed before me.' " From his superstore we have received one good gift after another. Moses gave us rules and regulations: Jesus, God's representative, gave us true love. No one has ever seen God, but the one faithful likeness who shares God's nature has shown us what God is like. (GAN pg 82 para 1)

Only Matthew and Luke tell the story of the birth of Jesus in Bethlehem. Mark seems almost to ignore the early life of Jesus, and the family do not come over particularly well in his Gospel, turning up to take Jesus home because they believe him to be mentally unhinged. There is another Gospel, however, that tells of the birth of Jesus in a completely different way. In Good As New, we call this Gospel 'Good News from Sources Close to Jesus', because we believe it stems from people who lived near Jerusalem and who knew Jesus intimately. Like the scholars C.H. Dodd, and John Robinson, I believe this Gospel to have appeared, at least in its first draft, at about the same time as Mark, that is 60 C.E. approximately. Read it in any translation and you will notice it has a very different style from the other Gospels. The fact that there is no account of Jesus' birth is one reason for thinking it an early Gospel. It was written, like Mark, at a time before the birth stories had begun to get around.

'Sources Close' (trad. John's Gospel) uses the language of theology and poetry to announce the appearance of God in the world. The theology and poetry is enhanced in most English translations, especially the King James Version of 1611. It is still good to hear it sometimes in the seventeenth century language, especially at Christmas. It helps on the feeling of wonder that is an essential part of the Christmas experience. It seems to fit the service of 'Nine Lessons and Carols' at King's College, Cambridge. However the Greek is simple, straightforward, common Greek, easy for the people of the first century to understand, even if Greek was only their second language. The wonder and the poetry are there alright, and the theology too, but it is all very down to earth.

If you want to follow the theology line, you need one of the standard commentaries which will elucidate the theological overtones and undertones of the word *logos*, translated usually as 'the Word'. It's a word specially chosen to have meaning for both Jewish and Gentile readers. For the Jews it would remind them of God speaking at the beginning and bringing about the universe—'Let there be light!'; for the Gentiles it would mean the reason sought by the philosophers and the relating principle holding everything together. For the Greeks 'light' meant the light of reason. But for the ordinary Joseph or Hector, it's all about God relating to us in the way we relate to one another, through speaking, talking, chatting. God seeks to communicate, just as we seek to communicate. The gospel writer announces that God is speaking and relating in a new way. This time it is not in the word of creation, though that is still there; nor in the words of the prophets, though John the Dipper is still on the scene; but as a human being, as someone of flesh and blood, like us.

'God spoke by means of a human being who shared a tent on our campsite'

That's exactly what the words in Greek mean. There was as much or more camping in those days than now. Most of the Jews who came to the many festivals at Jerusalem camped around the city. Refugees used tents, and so did the Arab nomad peoples who were never very far away. Only family, and those you regarded as your special friends, shared your tent, or pitched their tent next to yours on the same site. Had the author(-ess) of 'Sources Close' heard a rumour that Jesus was born in a makeshift tent in Bethlehem?

'The word became flesh'. God expressed Godself through the vehicle of a human being. Not half a human being! 'Sources Close' fights the Gnostic heresy that flesh is evil. When Jesus is on the cross he is speared by a sword that cut through his bladder. Out spurted a mixture of blood and urine. When Jesus sat down by the well in Samaria he was tired and thirsty. This was a real human being. God was born by the fleshly act of sexual intercourse, and came into the world via the vagina. There were those in the early days of the church who denied that God could have anything

to do with a real human body. It must have been some kind of show or fake. He couldn't have suffered like us. He couldn't have sexual feelings or go to the toilet. These views were condemned as heresy, and the earliest Christian scriptures try to combat it. But Gnosticism has remained a strong influence on the whole Christian community to this day. God not only made human bodies, and the bodies of all the animals let's not forget, but God used a body as an expression of the divine nature. We can share this nature, we can become family. But not by being physical descendants of Jesus. We don't know whether Jesus had any children. Probably not, despite Dan Brown. But his brothers and sisters probably had children. If there was any attempt in the early church to make it into a family thing, it was nipped in the bud. The idea of having something handed on from the first friends of Jesus, regrettably, did catch on. There are Christians today who believe you become a Christian, at least partly, by physical contact with someone who stands in a direct line of physical contact with the first apostles, who had touched Jesus. The Gospel writers would have been horrified by the idea of an 'Apostolic Succession' of priests, or that any particular church owed its authority to an unbroken link with the early church.

'Sources Close' does not provide a theology of the incarnation of God in Jesus. It simply says it happened. It would have been better if that's where it had been left, without all the confusing and contentious theology. But it was a difficult thing for a Jew to believe and still is. It is also difficult for many Christians and for Muslims. It was not a difficult idea for the Greeks and Romans whose gods were always paying visits to earth in human form, nor is it a problem for a Hindu who believes the gods who together represent one God, can appear in any form, including that of an animal.

I do not wish to push anyone in one direction or another on the question of the incarnation. I simply wish to say how I see it. I think it best if we each understand what happened in the life and death and resurrection of Jesus in our own way. That should be allowed. I also wish to suggest a place where people on opposite sides might be brought closer together. At Oxford University I attended the lectures of David Jenkins, later to become the notorious Bishop of Durham. He was a great lecturer in Patristics, the study of the works and the controversies of the early Greek Christian 'Fathers'. I came to the view in the end that it was a load of nonsense. The Fathers, devout and holy men (always men—part of the problem) played theological games and the losers were often burnt alive. The word 'love' does not appear in the creeds. They were formulated so that those who were heretical enough to be burnt alive could be identified.

The games revolved around the dual nature of Jesus—God and Man. This game has kept theologians preoccupied for two thousand years, and they've had a whale of a time, tying one another up in knots. The result for some has been a bi-polar Jesus and a bi-polar god.

The only thing we have to take on board, according to 'Sources Close' is that God has chosen to speak to us, to communicate with us by means of human flesh and blood. If we keep to that there should be no problem. If God is God, then God can be made known in any way God wants. God has done it in creation. The Hebrew scriptures tell us so. *'The heavens declare the glory of God'.* I was privileged to attend the lectures of Diarmud O'Murchu at the Othona Comunity in Dorset. He introduced us to the idea that God related to the human species throughout its evolution over seven million years. The point for us, for those of us who are homo sapiens of the civilization that began in the Fertile Crescent, is that God speaks to us in a way that is especially provided for our understanding. God speaks, God communicates, God seeks to relate to us. *We* muddy the waters.

'Sources Close' says that no one has seen God. Of course not. The being of God is beyond our reach of mind and of senses. Jews and Muslims are right about that. God is mystery. We should wonder and adore. We should take our shoes off our feet. The place where we stand, the environment in which we find ourselves, is holy ground. What 'Sources Close' says is that *to the extent* that as humans we are capable of understanding God, God has been shown to us in Jesus—on a level with us, on our campsite.

It's like the problem of translating from one language to another. You can never really understand a Russian novel unless first you learn Russian and learn to think and feel in Russian like a Russian. Hopeless for most of us. But a good translator can put it into English and will get you as close as an English speaker and thinker can get. God gives us a translation in the language of human flesh and blood. And according to 'Sources Close' the message we receive, loud and clear, is that 'God is Love'. Perhaps that's all we need to know. We can build our lives, we can build our faith on that. We can have a hope of heaven on that, because love never lets us go. It was at a lecture he gave after his retirement as Bishop of Durham, that David Jenkins concluded with these words,: 'God is. God is as seen in Jesus. That is the ground of our hope.'

Let All Mortal Flesh

Let all mortal flesh keep silence
lost in wonder at a child:
New born baby with potential,
seems so perfect, undefiled.
Though the weight of all the world hangs heavily,
'It's OK,' his father smiled.

Fragile flesh that knows its weakness
takes the challenges life brings.
Searching mind and working fingers,
open heart from which love springs.
Though the world can't see the God at work within,
with God's life creation sings.

Flesh and blood so bruised and broken
racked with pain upon the cross:
scorned, rejected, seems forsaken,
counted nothing more than dross.
Yet in Jesus' arms stretched out in selfless love,
God embraces pain and loss.

Born a poor child in a stable
challenging wealth's power to save.
Dying like a godless rebel
shows how violence can enslave.
Jesus shows God's chosen way of love,
ends the rule of pow'r in the grave.

[[*At Communion.*]]
Jesus then revealed as risen,
present here in symbols shared.
Bread and wine now speak of myst'ry,
love renewed and hope repaired.
In a world of climate change and bankruptcy,
God's way now in contrast declared.

[[After communion]]
So the wonder of a baby
after pain and strain of birth,
and the joy of resurrection
both affirm our human worth,
and the love of God that changes everything
is revealed on our patch of earth.]

[[Christmas morning]]
In the darkness light is shining,
new hope can be seen with the dawn.
Share the good news with your neighbours,
celebrate that Jesus is born.
Make the link from Christmas through to Easter Day;
God's son wakes up with a yawn.

(Simon Walkling 2008)

Chapter 6

~~~~~~~~~~~~~~~~

THE GOSPEL ACCORDING TO HARRY POTTER

**Exodus 7: 8-13; Matthew 2: 1-12
(Good As New page 125)**

I selected *Harry Potter and the Philosopher's Stone* for one Christmas holiday reading largely because the fundamentalists were telling us not to. I was not therefore surprised to find it full of gospel truth!

The Harry Potter books are for children, but have been read as much by adults as by their youngsters. They are adventure books about wizards and witches. I found Harry Potter easy reading and a very pleasant relief from the heavy theology or serious novels that I usually inflict on myself.

It's time the Christian Church recognized that the Holy Spirit did not lay down her pen at the year 90 or thereabouts. We need to take note of what she has been saying through the written word down the centuries, not only in works of piety, but in works of great literature and also in works of art and music. *Harry Potter* reminds us of gospel truths well displayed in the Christian scriptures, but which have grown pale due to over-familiarity.

1. Parts of the Bible do not appear to be very keen on **Magic**, which is the world of Harry Potter. These are the parts fundamentalists quote with their usual habit of choosing texts that bolster up their prejudices, turning a blind eye to anything that does not fit with those prejudices. Jeremiah told the people of his day, *'You must not listen to your.. sorcerers . . . . for they are prophesying a lie to you.'* (Jeremiah 27: 9). At that time the 'magic circle' gave different political advice to the monarch from that of Jeremiah—that's why he was opposed to them. In the Acts of the Apostles (Luke Part Two) we have the record of some Christians burning books of magic, though it is not made clear whether or not their actions were on the advice of the apostles. However, some magicians in the Bible have a better press. Moses was a magician and vied with the Egyptian magicians in performing magic tricks. The prophet Elisha made an axe float on water, and Isaiah made the shadow on a sundial go backwards! In the Christian scriptures magicians visit the child Jesus. Traditional translations have misled us by calling them 'Wise Men'. The Greek calls them 'Magi' which in the Greek lexicons is translated wizards, sorcerers, fortune-tellers, magicians. The Celts have always been keener on magic than the Anglo-Saxons. We have Merlin, the benign adviser to Arthur, the early Christian leader who sent his

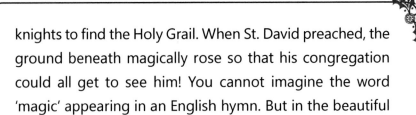

knights to find the Holy Grail. When St. David preached, the ground beneath magically rose so that his congregation could all get to see him! You cannot imagine the word 'magic' appearing in an English hymn. But in the beautiful hymn of T. Rowland Hughes we have the words

Tydi, a roddaist liw i'r wawr
A hud i'r machlud mwyn;

No problem in Welsh of speaking of the magic (hud) of the sunset, and of the dangers of losing the sense of that magic:

O! cadw ni rhag colli'r hud..

God save us from losing the magic! What is magic? It is a world of wonder. But much more, it is a world where there is no restriction on possibility. The two are linked. When you lose your sense of wonder at what has happened, you lose your ability to expect yet more wonders. When you are no longer surprised by the miracles of God's creation, from the beauty of the sunset to the birth of a baby, then you will fail to believe in the God of Jesus with whom *'all things are possible'*. Because the Magi were fascinated by the stars, they were also open to the possibility of God's arrival in the world.

This is how the story of Harry Potter begins:

When Mr and Mrs Dursley woke up on the dull, grey Tuesday our story starts, there was nothing about the cloudy sky outside to suggest that strange and mysterious things would soon be happening all over the country. Mr Dursley hummed as he picked out his most boring tie for work and Mrs Dursley gossiped away happily as she wrestled a screaming Dudley into his high chair. None of them noticed a large tawny owl flutter past the window . . . It was on the corner of the street that Mr Dursley noticed the first sign of something peculiar—a cat reading a map. For a second, Mr Dursley didn't realise what he had seen—then he jerked his head around to look again. There was a tabby cat standing on the corner of Privet Drive, but there wasn't a map in sight.

Mr. Dursley was a 'muggle'—a non-magic person. Because he didn't expect to see tabby cats reading maps, he wiped the sight from his consciousness. If we have no sense of magic, God's magic, and yes, the magic God has sprinkled around in the hearts and minds of humankind, then our lives will be humdrum and predictable and without sparkle. Bring back the magic—it's a Christian thing!

2. Reading the story of Harry Potter reminded me of a gospel word we do not use very often nowadays—**Providence.** Providence is an old word that means 'God looking after us'. Harry Potter is an orphan. He lives with his aunt and uncle who love their own son and spoil him rotten, but who ill-treat Harry because they sense that Harry is different. But Harry is watched over because he is a wizard, and when the time is ripe the wizards come to take him to the wizard's boarding school, Hogwarts. The school is presided over by Albus Dumbledore who keeps an eye on Harry in a very unobtrusive way. Harry is free to choose his own friends and even his own house by successfully directing the rather predestinarian 'sorting hat'. He is free even to break the school out-of-bounds rules and to embark on a dangerous adventure, but Dumbledore knows it all and sends him an anonymous present of an invisibility cloak at an opportune moment. Dumbledore also counsels Harry about the magic mirror that shows you what you desire most, but is a trap because it can lead to obsession.

God's Providence works in an environment of freedom. We are not prevented from breaking the rules, nor do we lose God's love thereby. God's helping hand is largely unseen, even anonymous. God gently deflects our gaze from what would harm us and oft-times protects us from the worst consequences of our naughty behaviour.

Jesus told us that God looks after the birds and the flowers in the countryside and notices when we are going bald. We need to recapture that sense of God's providence. It is the cure for anxiety!

3. The story of Harry Potter also confirms the Bible view of **good and evil.** Harry Potter, like the Bible, can be seen as a struggle between good and evil. There are good wizards and bad wizards; there are good forces and evil forces. Although Harry sometimes breaks the school rules, he sides with the weak and timorous against the school bullies. The Bible also makes it clear that goodness is not about keeping rules but about whether we are motivated by lust for power or by concern for others. The danger about seeing life as a battle about good and evil is that we look upon the two sides as being evenly matched. It can result in a religion that spends all its time fighting the devil and has no time to enjoy the 'life in all its fullness' Jesus defeated the devil in order to bring about. As in all the best stories, good wins the day against evil in *Harry Potter and the Philosopher's Stone.* But it's not just a matter of getting a good ending. Evil cannot win because it is no match for goodness, not because its magic is less powerful but because it has a tactical disadvantage. What prevented the evil wizard Voldemort from killing Harry as a baby, as he killed his parents, was the love Harry's mother showed in defending him. That love, symbolized by a scar on Harry's forehead, was what repulsed Voldemort's attack in this story. What love can do, and evil can never do, is make loving and dependable relationships. So that love will always have loving allies, whereas the only allies evil has are as selfish and self-seeking as itself. As Jesus said, the devil can't win, because *'a house that is divided against itself cannot stand.'* Voldemort depends on the baddie among the teaching staff, Professor Quirell, the man with two faces. Harry has on his side the love and loyalty of his small band of school friends who stay with him because he cares about *them*. That is why we never need to adopt aggressive or abusive tactics in evangelism. The victory of Jesus on the cross is not the defeat of one power by another. It is the defeat of power by the opposite of power—love.

4. In the first of the Harry Potter stories, the struggle is for the **Philosopher's Stone.** The stone is owned by a wizard called Nicholas Flamel, who has lived with its help for hundreds of years. Not only does it turn things to gold, but perpetuates life. It is lodged in a secure place in the school to prevent it from being stolen. Harry Potter and Co. help to prevent it being stolen by Voldemort. This is part of the conversation between Harry and Albus Dumbledore after it is all over:

'As for the stone', says Dumbledore, 'it has been destroyed'. Harry says, 'But that means he and his wife will die, won't they?' Dumbledore smiled at the look of amazement on Harry's face. 'To one as young as you, I'm sure it seems incredible, but to Nicholas and Perenelle, it is really like going to bed after a very long day. After all, to the well-organized mind, death is but the next great adventure.'

'Death is but the next great adventure.' And they tell us *Harry Potter* is not a Christian book! What a great thing to tell children and everybody else—the Good News that the last enemy 'death' has been defeated—the Good News of Jesus. What a pity that so many Christians still behave as if

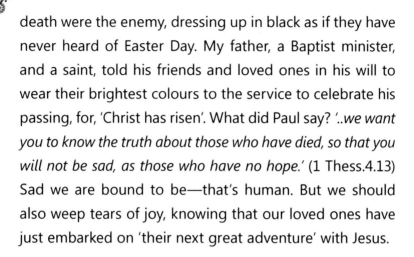

death were the enemy, dressing up in black as if they have never heard of Easter Day. My father, a Baptist minister, and a saint, told his friends and loved ones in his will to wear their brightest colours to the service to celebrate his passing, for, 'Christ has risen'. What did Paul say? *'..we want you to know the truth about those who have died, so that you will not be sad, as those who have no hope.'* (1 Thess.4.13) Sad we are bound to be—that's human. But we should also weep tears of joy, knowing that our loved ones have just embarked on 'their next great adventure' with Jesus.

I have read the remainder of the Harry Potter books with equal profit. In the last but one book, Professor Dumbledore makes the supreme sacrifice, giving his life for those he loves. As I predicted, the theme of Resurrection appears in the last volume. I believe that the Harry Potter series is an improvement as a Christian allegory on C.S. Lewis's 'The Lion, The Witch and the Wardrobe', and may prove to be the greatest Christian allegory since 'A Pilgrim's Progress' by John Bunyan. J.K. Rowling did not reveal her commitment as a Christian until after all the books had been published. A very shrewd tactic! Read the books for yourself. They contain words from God.

Chapter 7

EVERY STAR SHALL SING A CAROL

Sidney Carter was one of the great hymn/song writers of the twentieth century. He was so good that some widely used hymn books give him a miss. We can't have people thinking too adventurously, or letting their imaginations run wild! 'Every star shall sing a carol' is more than a pretty piece with a haunting tune. Carter has something serious and thought-provoking to say. He was attempting to get Christians and others to come to grips with the God of the 'Space Age'.

Every star shall sing a carol?

The nearest star to us is called (by us) Alpha Centauri. It is over 25 million miles away (4.3 light years). It is the *nearest* star. I have not yet heard whether any planets have been discovered around it, or if so, whether any of them has the right conditions for life. Our sun is one of the least significant of the 100 million stars in our galaxy, the Milky Way. The Milky Way is just one of millions of galaxies. The mind doesn't boggle—it gives up! Given such vast numbers it seems unlikely that we are the only intelligent beings to exist. But despite Doctor Who and science fiction, contacting them and meeting up with them is probably a physical impossibility.

My friend Revd. Bill Samuel was at one time my adviser as the Moderator of the United Reformed Church in Wales. He lost his faith before he died. He told me that the realization of the size of the universe by modern science had shaken his faith. He was probably reflecting the feelings of many people today for whom the God of the Christian religion, confined as that God appears to be to our little planet for a fraction of its history, does not seem to square with the immensity of time and space. Yet the problem is not a new one. The poet who composed Psalm 8 wrote:

'When I look at the sky, which you have made, at the moon and the stars, which you have set in their places, what is humankind that you think about us; mere mortals that you care for us?'

God has no size; no beginning or end. God is infinite in all directions—the direction of the larger and the direction of the smaller. That has always been beyond the understanding of human beings. If we were to put a limit to God, God would not be God.

But what if there are other intelligent beings in the universe? Where do they stand in relation to God? *Every* star shall sing a carol. If such intelligent beings exist, God is their God as well.

> *'Who can tell what other cradle*
> *High above the Milky Way,*
> *Still may rock the King of Heaven*
> *On another Christmas day?'*

Just suppose that intelligent life exists on another planet. It is unlikely to be humanoid. They may not have eyes or ears, or flesh or bones like us. How will God relate to that life? The God we believe in, the God of love, came as close to us as possible. In some mysterious way we cannot understand, this God entered and shared our human life. The creator became the creature, or something like that. The baby in the feeding trough is 'Immanuel', 'God with us'. Is it too fanciful to suppose that God would do something similar for any other intelligent and sensitive beings who like us look up and wonder at the stars? It is then reasonable to suppose that there are, have been or will be other Christmas days. I don't find that a disturbing idea. I find it awesome!

But the carol continues past Christmas day:

> *'Who can count how many crosses,*
> *Still to come or long ago,*
> *Crucify the King of Heaven . . . ?'*

God is love. Love means freedom. Love means invitation to love in return. Invitation, never compulsion. There exists the possibility of rejection. The freedom given or acquired, necessary for a loving relationship, means freedom to behave badly, to lust for excesses of pleasure, wealth or power, to squabble, to fight, to wound, to kill. A God who truly loves must allow this freedom. But the anguish caused by freedom abused will become God's own anguish multiplied. The idea of other intelligent life on other planets leads to the possibility of their being other Calvaries. We know of a cross. The cross shape seems to speak to us of God's suffering in a special way, with the arms outstretched to embrace and to save. On another planet the form of suffering might be different. There are endless ways of torture, endless ways of death. Who can tell?

'Who can tell what other body
He will hallow for his own?
I will praise the son of Mary,
Brother of my blood and bone.'

We know God as Jesus, the son of Mary. We wonder, what will his, or her name be on planet 'X'. What are God's parents' names, supposing the beings have parents in our sense? What will be her employment or role in society? Who will be her special friends? What stories will she tell, what wonders will she perform, what acts of kindness? Who can tell? I will praise the son of Mary and Joseph, fully human like myself.

Today is Christmas Day on Planet Earth. We celebrate 'God with us' in Jesus, though even on this planet other faiths celebrate 'God with us' in alternative ways. We have had our invitation to the divine Christmas Party, and so have they. All are invited by God to enter into an eternal relationship of love. We are given the freedom to reject God or to befriend God. We can ignore God, or we can sing a carol.

> *'Every star and every planet,*
> *Every creature high or low,*
> *Come and praise the King of Heaven*
> *By whatever name you know.'*

Part Two

ADVENT SERIES

John Henson & Ray Vincent.

THIS IS THE ADVENT SEASON

This is the Advent season
When we devote some time
To use imagination
And visit days long gone;
Times hidden deep in darkness
And written records missed,
Where we depend on diggers
And anthropologists.

God surely did not shun them.
Those ancestors of ours,
Who lived in caves and forests
Closer to nature's powers.
They fashioned tools and broaches
And though they lived short lives,
They made graves for their loved ones,
And through all ills survived.

The moment they got writing,
Recording first on stone,
They showed they had religion
And did not walk alone.
They sensed a divine presence
Within them and around;
Someone was there to help them
If they could just be found.

Then in a tiny corner
Of this world's wide expanse,
There was a man called Abram
Who met God in a trance.
His God was no wild monster,
But looking for a friend;
In spite of many downturns,
They friendshiped to the end.

And Moses and Elijah
Found God upon a mount;
And Amos in some blossom,
And Joel in a fount;
Isaiah in a baby
He named Immanuel,
To indicate that maybe
God might in nappies* dwell.

It all seemed rather puzzling,
This presence without form,
A now forgotten child's game
Of "Now you're getting warm".
And then there were some pointers,
The 'chosen', 'servant', 'lamb',
And finally a feed trough
In uptown Bethlehem.

_____

*   USA diapers.

And others too came searching,
Some seers from Persia far,
A pagan Roman soldier
Who put his trust right there;
Some Greeks with their deep thinking,
A devotee of Baal,
A madman from Transjordan
Who turned the neighbours pale.

Yet God remains still hidden,
We still expect and wait;
Christmas again is coming,
But never quite a fact.
And God may be embodied
In other Bethlehems,
And queerer wise folk offer
Their perfumes and their gems.

(John Henson Advent 2011 Tune: Cruger)

Chapter 8

PRESENTS IN THE FAMILY

John Henson

Presents for Rebecca: Genesis 24: 10-24

The family of Abraham is one of the oldest families in the world, with an unbroken history for about 3,000 years. We are adopted members of it. I don't know very much about my great-grandparents, except that one could only speak Welsh and another was drowned when swimming naked at Ogmore. But, thanks to the Bible, I know a lot about my distant ancestors who lived in the fertile crescent, the 'Cradle of Civilization'. I know that they gave one another presents, and what they gave.

The seniors of the family were Abraham and Sarah. Their son was Isaac. The time came for them to arrange his marriage as was the custom. But they didn't fancy any of the local girls in Palestine, so decided to send back home to their country of origin. Some Asians do the same today. Abraham sent his trusted servant Eliezer back to northern Iraq where he still had relatives. Eliezer (let's call him Les) went with ten camels. What did he need ten camels for? He could only ride one at a time. The object was to impress. Les arrived at his destination at about evening time, took his camels to the well, watched and prayed. Rebecca, a beautiful young woman, came out of her house, gave Les a drink and watered his camels. Les decided this was the one for Isaac. He gave Rebecca an expensive gold ring for her to wear in her nose and two large gold bracelets, one for each arm. Negotiations with the family followed and the marriage was arranged. A lovely story, you must read it all to get the full flavour.

On first reading it seems that this is a story in which Les identified a good wife for Isaac because Rebecca so readily performed an act of kindness to a stranger. I don't want to spoil the story for you, but I'm going to. The whole village were looking out when Les arrived with his camels. At once the race was on. Rebecca got there first. The family would no doubt have been happy to give her to Les himself if all those camels had been his, never mind if he was getting on a bit in years. When Rebecca came back in and showed her new jewellery to the other members of the family, that clinched it. It helped, of course, that the prospective bridegroom was a distant cousin.

Arranged marriages are often more permanent than those where the parties 'fall in love'. Arranged marriages do not rely on sex or the emotions for success, but on ideals of loyalty and duty. But the marriage between Isaac and Rebecca was not a happy marriage. Rebecca was a bright young thing; Isaac was a bore. The craftiness with which she got her man was later used to deceive him when she wanted to promote the interests of her favorite son Jacob against those of his twin brother Esau, his father's favorite.

So much for Les's expensive presents and Rebecca's apparent kindness! They produced a marriage, but failed to produce a relationship. The Bible said it a long time before the Beatles: 'Money can't buy me love'. So here's question one for you to think about when you buy your presents this Christmas time, or any other time. What do you hope to achieve by the present you give? Many relationships begin with an impressive exchange of presents. But what relationships require is a sharing of mind and heart, openness and honesty in the getting-to-know-you process. And do we really think that the bigger the present we give somebody, the more we are likely to obtain their long-term love and loyalty? Do we think our children will be more endeared to us, the bigger the presents? Some parents obviously think so. Poor dabs!

Presents for Esau: Genesis 33: 1-10

Our second story follows the consequences of the unhappy marriage between Isaac and Rebecca. They had twin boys, Esau and Jacob. Esau was the elder. Esau was Isaac's favourite; Jacob was Rebecca's favourite. Rebecca concocted a cunning plan whereby Jacob diddled Esau out of his lawful inheritance. Jacob was forced to flee his brother's wrath, back to the old country to the home of his uncle Laban, Rebecca's brother. Laban was as crooked as Rebecca and Jacob. Jacob spent seven years working for Laban's lovely daughter Rachel and got Leah, his less lovely daughter, instead. Then he had to work another seven years for Rachel whom he truly loved. Fourteen years waiting for your loved-one. That's love! Jacob worked a few tricks on Laban to get his own back and found himself having to run away again with nowhere to go except back to brother Esau. What sort of reception would he get? More cunning required. First he sent wave after wave of presents for Esau, *'two hundred female goats and twenty males, two hundred female sheep and twenty males, thirty milk camels with their young, forty cows and ten bulls, twenty female donkeys and ten males.'* (32:14) A fortune for those days. Then just in case even this did not do the trick, he sent his wives, concubines and their children on first. Esau, always ruled by his heart rather than his head, was deeply moved and said things like 'Oh, you really shouldn't . . . . I couldn't possibly . . .'. He accepted the gifts anyway. But he was genuinely pleased to see his brother and they both had a good cry.

This is a moving story of reconciliation between two brothers. The presents played a part in the reconciliation, though it seems Esau would have been happy to forgive his brother without them. But we mustn't think that Jacob was simply up to his old tricks. He was not the same person he was fourteen years ago when he did the dirty on Esau. In between he had met God and like Abraham his grandfather and Isaac his father he developed a relationship with God. He had seen heaven opened at Bethel and he had wrestled with God at Peniel. Yes, he was the same cool-headed businessman. But now he had a conscience as well. And he had a heart like Esau, and a wife who inspired his love. It was not all self, self, self. He knew the joy of giving. The gifts he gave to Esau he might have resented having to make in the long ago. Now he rather enjoyed it. It gave him a thrill to see somebody else's happiness. In this old story from the Hebrew scriptures there appears one of the most significant texts in the whole Bible. Jacob said to his brother Esau *'No, please, . . . accept my gift. To see your face is for me like seeing the face of God'* (33:11). Jacob has discovered that the face of God can be recognized in another human being, and that loving God and loving your brother are as near being identical as makes no difference. To give in a spirit of open heartedness and genuine love to someone who is really appreciative is a Godly thing. To be reconciled to brother, sister, friend, fellow-human; to forgive from the heart—that is what God likes to see.

A Present for Joseph: Genesis 37: 1-4

Jacob produced a big family. From his two wives and two concubines he produced twelve sons and at least one daughter. But from his beloved Rachel only two sons, Joseph and Benjamin. Rachel died giving birth to Benjamin. Jacob was heart-broken. His love for his wife he re-directed to the little boys she had given him, particularly Joseph the elder who had Rachel's good looks. You have to be very careful when you have more than one child to avoid favoritism. It's natural but it's not good. We let Iestyn watch his chosen programme on telly once when it was Gareth's turn to choose (or was it the other way round?). It was a long time before we heard the last of it.

Jacob should have known better from the memory of his rivalry with Esau. But he couldn't help himself. It was Joseph's birthday. Joseph rather liked dressing up. So Jacob gave him a coat in the latest fashion, with long flowing sleeves, all colours of the rainbow. Where did he get it from? More than likely from one of the caravan traders who regularly passed that way. It obviously cost a bomb. A famous coat, celebrated in a twentieth century musical.

It was a fatal present. Joseph's brothers were so envious they attempted to kill him. One took pity on him and sold him into slavery, which was not much better. Joseph became Prime Minister of Egypt. But that in turn led to the family moving to Egypt and after a few generations they all became slaves.

So we are warned that there is more to present giving than letting your feelings take over and splashing out. Present-giving can be dangerous, especially present-giving on a lavish scale. We say it's the thought that counts, but we only half believe it. We want to give something special and we like receiving something special, and in our materialistic civilisation 'special' relates to the price tag.

The size and expense of the presents we give one another at Christmas is sinful. Sinful because we fall into the trap of putting price tags on our friendships and relationships, and sinful because it embodies a flaunting of our wealth in a world in which so many are in need of the basic necessities of life. Have you ever imagined what it must be like to walk around the shopping area of a large town or city at Christmastime if your only form of income is 'the social' and you have no proper home, family or friends? And you see all the shoppers, day after day, staggering beneath the weight of their Christmas presents and Christmas goodies. I've walked side by side down Queen Street in Cardiff with a homeless person and felt the anger. We Christians moan about the commercializing of Christmas. But what are we going to do about it? If the trend is going to be reversed it has to start with us who should know the true meaning of Christmas. It's not going to start anywhere else.

I have made covenants with members of my family and friends. I promise not to buy you a present if you promise not to buy me one—and this means we care for one another *and* for those in need. One of my friends and I agreed for many years to buy one another presents costing £1 only. It's a challenge. It means you really have to hunt, get to the charity shops early before their stocks are gone, and you have to use your imagination. It's the thought that counts, but I've had some interesting presents that way.

If Christians don't behave like Christians at Christmas time, who will? We don't have to be miserable just because we are not spending, spending, spending. It can be joyful and diverting to see how little we can spend and to discover other ways of expressing our love at the same time. Let's spend less on presents this Christmas and let's show more love.

Chapter 9

THE GIFTS OF THE RICH

Ray Vincent

1 Kings 10: 1-13

Solomon, the son of David, was a king of legendary wealth and wisdom. The story is told in the First Book of Kings of how the Queen of Sheba came to visit him. The Queen of Sheba is a mysterious figure, not known outside this story. Sheba may have been the same as Seba, the land of the Sabaeans, an area in southern Arabia around what is now Yemen, possibly spreading across the straits to the African coast of Ethiopia. It was a trading nation, known in more modern times for the port of Aden, and of proverbial wealth. Psalm 72 talks of *'the kings of Sheba and Seba'* bringing gifts to the king of Israel. Generally Seba is linked with Egypt and Ethiopia as a symbol of wealth and power. In Isaiah 45:14 we read of *'the wealth of Egypt and the merchandise of Ethiopia, and the Sabaeans, tall of stature'*.

However, the main point of this story is to highlight the wealth of Solomon. The Queen of Sheba came with presents: *'camels bearing spices, and very much gold, and precious stones'*. This giving of presents by one ruler to another is a very ancient custom. It was, and still is, often very ostentatious and competitive—just like Christmas presents today! Things haven't changed. It's still the people who are already rich who get the most expensive presents.

Today the ostentation is not just for kings and rulers, but reaches us ordinary people, caught up in the fever of commercialism. We are exposed to constant adverts. New products keep appearing, creating new 'needs'. Until the recent 'credit crunch' we were all being encouraged to buy, buy, buy and put it all on the credit card. Christmas is often a time of great anxiety for people who find it hard to make ends meet. It is also a time of loneliness and the feeling of being left out for those who don't have cosy homes to decorate and happy families to spend Christmas with. Even for the well off, it is a hectic time of struggling through the shops and racking our brains about what to give to people who have everything but still expect a present.

Is Christmas really a pleasure anymore? And does it have anything to do with Jesus? And if we don't like it, what can we do? In recent years, a Saturday shortly before Christmas has been designated 'Buy Nothing Day'! People put on light-hearted demonstrations in shopping malls, set up stalls giving out free tea outside Starbucks, or free sandwiches outside McDonalds. Suggestions are made for ways we can give our time, not our money. So much more creative and more fun than the Christmas many of us are getting a bit tired of.

We sometimes talk as if God is a great king worthy of all the richest gifts. The Magicians gave Jesus gold, frankincense and myrrh. Down through the ages great cathedrals have been built in his name and richly furnished by powerful princes and wealthy merchants. The Christian religion has produced some of the world's finest art and most glorious music. Christians have often thought in terms of 'nothing but the best for God'. But what kind of 'best' does God really want?

Psalm 50 is a protest against the cult of sacrifice. Why should God want all these bulls and goats to be offered up to him, it asks. *'For every wild animal of the forest is mine, the cattle on a thousand hills . . . If I were hungry, I would not tell you, for the world and all that is in it is mine.'*

So what kind of present does 'the God who has everything' want? The answer in this psalm is *'offer to God a sacrifice of thanksgiving . . . Call on me in the day of trouble'*. Thankfulness and trust are the gifts God appreciates most from us. What do loving parents who give everything to their children want in return? Surely the most precious return is their children's love and trust, the confidence that they will be the ones their children turn to if ever they are in trouble.

Jesus goes a step further. In the story he tells in Matthew 25 he talks of people who served him in all kinds of ways. They ask in genuine ignorance, *'when did we ever give you a good meal or stand you a drink? When did we have you in our house or give you clothes? We don't remember you being ill or visiting you in prison'*. Then Jesus, the Leader, the Complete Person, will say *'Believe me, when you did these things for people most think not worth the trouble, you did them for me. They are my family'*. Jesus identifies himself with the poorest, and says 'You want to honour me? Honour them!'

Chapter 10

PRESENTS AND LOVE

John Henson

1 Samuel 1:1-28 & 2: 18-21.

One of my favourite preachers was the radical and controversial United Reformed minister Douglas Bale. On one of his visits to Pontypridd we were going through a period of following the Lectionary (fixed Bible readings). Doug found himself having to preach on the story of Hannah from the first book of Samuel. He began by saying that it's time we realized that some of the stories in the Bible are irrelevant to us today and that we shouldn't bother with them. Then he said that the story of Hannah is one of them. I certainly agree that there is much is the Bible that we must drop, simply because it does not accord with the mind of Christ. We no longer stone adulterers as we are commanded in the Bible, because Jesus refused to. Doug was wrong about the story of Hannah. It's a very relevant story. It's the story of a woman who was stigmatized; it's the story of a 'modern man'; it's the story of how one of the hymns we still sing today came to be written; it's a story of child abuse; and it's a story which contains a present. Is that relevant enough?

A woman who was stigmatized.

Hannah was a young woman under a stigma. She had failed to bear children for her husband. If you were in that category you were in trouble in those days. You were labelled 'barren'. It was always the woman's fault. She was under a curse, shunned, derided. Human society has always enjoyed stigmatizing people. The Church has often joined in and sometimes been responsible for introducing the stigma. There are many ancient churches in Europe where you can still find the special window for the lepers to look through to watch the service. Different societies have chosen different groups to stigmatize, but nearly all societies pick on somebody. Many people, many churches indeed, shun the mentally disabled or the extremely physically handicapped or disfigured. One church where I have preached lost half its congregation because of the regular attendance of people from the nearby home for the mentally disabled. They sang very enthusiastically very out of tune, but otherwise were not a real problem. They made people feel uncomfortable. Being a Christian isn't about being comfortable. If that's what you think, it's time to think again. Jesus made the marginalized his priority targeting. He even embraced the lepers and went home to lunch with them. His business is our business.

A 'Modern Man'.

Hannah's husband was called Elkanah. I call him Len. He had two wives, Hannah and Penny. We are told that Penny would torment and humiliate Hannah *'because the Lord had kept her childless'*. Notice how she used religion as the whip with which to beat the despised Hannah. Some Christians think the Bible is for bashing other people on the head with. One day Len asked Hannah why she was crying. You can see him putting his arm around her as he said, *'Why are you always so sad? Don't I mean more to you than ten sons?'* 'Never mind about the children, we've got one another!' In adopting that attitude Len was going against all the prejudice of his day. Wives were for producing children, not for having relationships with! Len's feelings were for his wife in her sorrow and sense of isolation. Len was a modern man. You can almost hear him saying 'Come on, let's do the washing up together; you wash, I'll wipe'. Len wore a ribbon for barren wives. He identified himself with them and empathized with their stigma. He treated Hannah not as a barren woman but as a human being. That's how Jesus saw people—not as saints or sinners, not as insiders or outsiders, not as rich or poor, high class or low class, strong or weak, respectable or not respectable, but human beings. It should never be forgotten that the first citizen of God's New World on Good Friday was a convicted criminal, but in the sight of Jesus one of the precious souls for whom he was dying.

An old song.

One of my interests over the years has been the updating of old hymns to enable them to be sung honestly and joyfully in this new millennium. This is nothing novel. Very few of the hymns we sing, which we think of as old hymns, are in their original version. They have often been revised many times over the centuries Did you know that 'The Magnificat' is not Mary's song? It was first sung by Hannah. Mary simply adapted it to her own circumstances. Mary sang it for joy at the news that her cousin Lisa (Elizabeth) had conceived. Lisa was another 'barren', 'stigmatized' woman like Hannah. Indeed the song was likely used, from the time of Hannah on, in services of thanksgiving when the barren had conceived. In both Hannah and Mary's version the song is surprisingly not so much about having babies as about revolution. It's about a changed world where all stigmas are done away with. Hannah sings, 'He lifts the poor from the dust and raises the needy from their misery. He makes them companions of princes and puts them in the places of honour.' Mary sings, *'He has put down the mighty from their seat: and has exalted the humble and meek. He has filled the hungry with good things: and the rich he has sent empty away.'* People who have been stigmatized like Hannah and Lisa are hypersensitive to the burden of the stigma carried by others. Once you start seeing people as people and identify with their needs, you will, like Jesus and his mother Mary, become a revolutionary and probably get yourself into trouble. The first Christians were described as people who were 'turning the world upside down'.

A case of child abuse.

In order to conceive Hannah did a deal with God. No one should ever try to do that. You cannot bargain with God. It doesn't work; it always goes wrong. God is not up for special offers, or bribes. But Hannah was desperate. *'If you give me a son, I promise that I will dedicate him to you for his whole life'* (v 11) That meant that as soon as the child was weaned he would be taken to the House of God, where he would stay to his dying day (v22). That was a terrible bargain and one we can be sure God would not have wanted. Again we can reject such horrible ideas by looking at Jesus. In Jesus God demonstrated the importance of a mother's love. Jesus stayed at home with his mother until he was about thirty. That's why his stories are full of pictures of his mother about the house, baking the bread, grinding at the mill, sweeping the room. Samuel was torn from his mother's love before he had chance to get to know her and was put in the charge of Eli at the shrine at Shiloh. Eli was old, half blind, notoriously a bad parent whose two sons had turned out to be a thoroughly bad lot. The main operation in the shrine where this young child would be expected to assist was the grisly business of animal sacrifice. When I was about twelve and in a Secondary Modern School, since I had failed the 11+, my parents considered sending me to a private school—Mill Hill, then a Baptist foundation. Many of my father's colleagues in the ministry were doing the same at that time. My parents were sensitive enough to realise that I was a home boy and that I would have been destroyed as a person if they had sent me away. I later followed the careers of the sons of my father's friends. They all went wrong in some way or another. I'm not totally against boarding schools provided they are the genuine choice of the pupils concerned. My nephew went to a Methodist mixed boarding school and was very happy. He was an only child, had no friends and wanted to be with other youngsters. It worked for him because it was his choice.

We have this Sunday School picture of Samuel, the pure holy young child, instructed by Eli, listening for God's word and so on. In fact he turned out to be quite a nasty piece of work. His fierce loyalty to God, as he understood it, could not be faulted. He was politically astute and realised when it was time for Saul to be replaced by David as King of Israel. But when Saul wanted out of humanity to spare his fellow king, Agag, after defeating him in a battle, Samuel took an axe and hacked Agag in pieces. Saul was a mixed up kid, but he was a nicer man than Samuel. All the criminal offenders whom I have befriended over the past twenty years have had one thing in common. They were all separated from their mothers either by death or family break-up at an early age, and in some cases brought up by vicious and abusive fathers. There is more than one kind of abuse and today, and no doubt at all Samuel would be identified by a psychiatrist as a victim of abuse. We must realise that not all religion is good. Just because someone does something from a religious motive or can quote the Bible to back them up, does not mean they are doing what God would want. Much of the religion on offer today, including the Christian religion, does not reflect the mind of Jesus and we should be on our guard. Read the gospels over and over and over again, without blinkers, each time as if you were reading them for the first time. The Mind of Christ is the defence against bad religion.

The Present

So finally there is this sad little picture of Hannah, the mother, once a year visiting her boy and bringing with her the little robe that possibly she herself had made on her little hand loom or got a neighbour to make—each year a little bigger. No, I don't agree with Doug Bale about this story. In fact most of the Bible has something to say to us. But sometimes its message is about what we should *not* do rather than about what we should do. Parents, and friends: no amount of presents, however big, however lovingly selected and carefully packed, can make up for the present of *time* spent with those you love. One member of my family phoned me to ask what I wanted for Christmas. After a pause for thought I said 'Please take me out for a meal, just you and me together. If you can't afford to pay the lot we'll go halves, except that you can pay an extra pound and that will be your pound present to me. I have already bought your present which cost me exactly £1'. Why do we send cards if we have phones? It's much better to hear somebody's voice. It's giving them time. Much better still better, arrange to visit them or meet them—later in the year if things are too busy at the moment, but fix it in the diary and let it be like the law of the Medes and Persians. Did Hannah ever regret her foolish promise to God? Did she ever shed a tear? You bet she did—more tears than she shed when she had no child at all. Let's not be foolish. Let's give the best present this Christmastime—the present of ourselves.

Chapter 11

THE GIFTS OF THE POOR

Ray Vincent

1 Kings 17: 1-24.

In 1 Kings 17 we have a story about the prophet Elijah. It was a time of famine. There had been no rain for many months. Elijah, like everyone else, was short of food. Where could he go for help? The place to which he was guided was not a palace, or even a farm with some grain in store, but the home of a poor widow!

He met the widow at the town gate, and asked for food. What was she to do? All she had was a handful of flour and a few drops of oil—just enough for one last meal for herself and her young son before they starved to death. This man was obviously a prophet, a man of God. It was a sacred duty to feed him, but how could she? Nevertheless, she did. She fed him not only that day, but for many more days—and somehow the flour and the oil never ran out.

However, some time later things took a sudden turn for the worse. Her son became ill and died. For a long time she had felt blessed by the prophet's presence, but now things had gone terribly wrong. What kind of blessing was this? She reacted, as bereaved people often do, with a mixture of anger and guilt. A superstitious fear took hold of her. The presence of a man of God could be threatening rather than blessing. Perhaps by letting him into her home she had attracted God's attention and was now being punished for her sins.

Elijah, who had nothing to give, could only share her puzzlement and anger, and express it to God. Then another miracle happened. Elijah lay on top of the child and prayed earnestly to God, and the child came back to life.

Did either of these things happen just as the story says? Were they 'miracles' in the sense in which we usually mean the word? These are old stories, part of the folklore of Israel. Like most old stories, they are probably exaggerations of real events. Perhaps Elijah made a general prophecy that food and oil would not run out until the rain came—in other words rain would come very soon—and maybe this story was woven out of that. Perhaps the boy was not dead, but very ill, and after Elijah's prayer and loving attention he revived. It may help some people to hold onto the belief that there was something supernatural here, and to say that if the Bible says it, it must be true. But however that may be, we know that things like that don't generally happen in our experience.

Nevertheless this story reminds us of some pretty wonderful facts about life, facts that in a sense are miracles. We often find that poor people are more generous than rich people. Europeans who visit communities in Africa that are just one step away from starvation are often amazed by the generosity, and the cheerfulness, of their hospitality. We often find too that if we are open to other people and their needs, our slender resources, whether material or emotional, can go an incredibly long way. If we have no wealth to give, miracles can happen when we share our poverty

I once visited a member of my church who was an alcoholic, and he told me how he was doing his best to help another member who was depressive. As I listened to him it suddenly struck me that this is what the Church is about, and it's miraculous!

At Christmas time, when we are all trying to show our love by giving expensive presents, we need to remember that in the end it's not the presents that count, but the love and the sharing. We miss something of this by being rich. One way we try to cope with it is to give donations to charity or buy charity cards. 'Charity' is big business at Christmas these days. It helps to salve our conscience, and it does a lot of good for people who are in need. In fact, there should be more of it. How about giving up a little of your cosy family Christmas to help at a shelter for homeless people? It's very rewarding, and more fun than many of our boring family Christmases!

But charity is not the real answer. One reason why it is hard for rich people to enter the kingdom of heaven is that, even if we are well-meaning, inequality of wealth corrupts our relationship with the poor. We can never be on equal terms as human beings. We give what we choose to give, they accept what they have no choice but to accept.

Often, when faced with a plea for help, I have asked myself. 'What would Jesus do?' Unfortunately, the answer is obvious. Jesus wouldn't have had to make this decision, because he had no money anyway. He went around with nothing, only himself, to give. Like his disciples later, he could have said, 'I have no silver and gold, but such as I have I give you'. Rich or poor, the best thing we have to give is ourselves.

The gifts of the poor are more precious than the gifts of the rich. There is a story in Luke 21 about Jesus watching people throw their gifts into the temple collection box. He drew attention to a poor widow who put in two small copper coins, and said that she had given more than all the rich people, because she had given all she had.

The story of the feeding of the five thousand is a beautiful example of this, especially as John tells it (John 6). The five loaves and two fishes were offered by a young lad. They

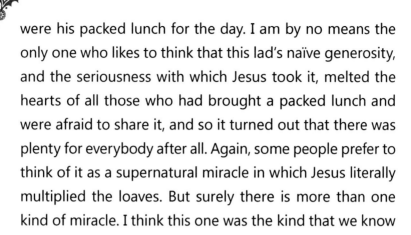

were his packed lunch for the day. I am by no means the only one who likes to think that this lad's naïve generosity, and the seriousness with which Jesus took it, melted the hearts of all those who had brought a packed lunch and were afraid to share it, and so it turned out that there was plenty for everybody after all. Again, some people prefer to think of it as a supernatural miracle in which Jesus literally multiplied the loaves. But surely there is more than one kind of miracle. I think this one was the kind that we know could well happen in our own experience, and for me that makes it somehow more inspiring and heart-warming.

In the Christmas story there are no rich people dispensing charity (the Magicians came later, and in any case they were not kings: perhaps they too were quite poor, and the gifts they gave were small and symbolic). There was someone who offered a feeding trough. The shepherds had nothing to offer but their adoration. The idea that one of them brought a lamb is a sentimental addition to the story. The whole story is of God coming into the world in poverty, not dispensing great gifts, but giving the greatest gift of all—God's self. This is what love is, and this is what God is.

Chapter 12

PRESENTS AND PRIDE

John Henson (preached on AIDS Sunday)

I Samuel 18: 1-4 2 Kings 5: 9-19

Tonight we think about two pairs of people who exchanged presents, with very different intentions and with very different effect. We shall learn, I hope, something about the way we should treat one another and how we should give and accept presents.

The friendship between David and Jonathan is one of the most famous friendships in history. It was a startling relationship in more ways than one. The most startling thing about it was that one was a king's son, the heir to the throne, while the other was a shepherd boy, the youngest and therefore least important of eight brothers belonging to a farming family in a poor district. He practised the harp while looking after the sheep, was talent-spotted and played before king Saul. Thus Jonathan and David were as far apart as they could possibly be in status and wealth. David depended on the king's patronage entirely for his livelihood, was virtually a slave, whereas Jonathan had the means to purchase anything that money and royal influence could buy.

When David and Jonathan swore eternal friendship, Jonathan showered David with gifts—his own royal robe, his armour, his sword, bow and belt—and persuaded his father to give him a commission in the army. David gave Jonathan nothing, since he had nothing to give. Yet the friendship comes across as a friendship of equals. The disparity between what they had to offer in terms of material things did not matter. Jonathan, without stinting, gave David the very best he had to offer; David accepted the gifts without embarrassment and without any feeling of inadequacy.

The other pair we read about were both famous and influential people, each in his own way. Norman (Naaman) was the commander of the dreaded Syrian army and one of the king of Syria's most valuable ministers. He was affected by a stubborn skin disease, which may have been leprosy or something less serious, but it came to the same thing in those days. There was only one way of dealing with such things—isolation and exclusion from society. His whole life was about to fall in ruins. Those who became HIV positive or contracted AIDS in the 1980s and 90s knew exactly how he felt. It is not so much the diminished life expectancy and the restraints that accompany ill health, but the loneliness and isolation, and the dependence on the kindliness, compassion and tolerance of others, which could not always be taken for granted in our civilization any more than it could be in the Ancient World. The world hasn't changed that much.

Norman was sent by his king to the famous prophet and healer in Israel next door to Syria. The two countries were not on friendly terms and fought wars from time to time. The prophet's name was Elis (Elisha). He was one of the old school of prophets, strict, intolerant, everything by the rule book. If this man was ill, it was his own fault; God was punishing him, no doubt for his false religion and his heathen life-style.

When Norman called at Elis' door, Elis refused to come out and deal with him personally. He sent his servant in and out with messages. He didn't want to catch anything nasty. Elis also had no time for foreigners. God's people must not be affected by pagan, secular culture. He intended to keep himself pure and holy in every sense of the word. He did, however, from his position of moral and religious superiority, send Norman a prescription. Norman should have a good wash!

Norman was desperate, but like Elis he was proud— proud of his race and country. There were better rivers for washing in back home than the river Jordan; he was proud of his status as the king's right hand man. He was incensed by the ignorance and impudence of this narrow-minded

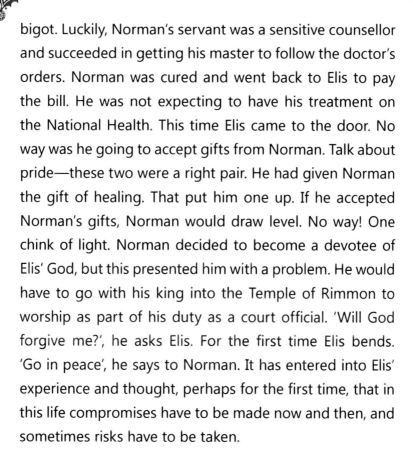

bigot. Luckily, Norman's servant was a sensitive counsellor and succeeded in getting his master to follow the doctor's orders. Norman was cured and went back to Elis to pay the bill. He was not expecting to have his treatment on the National Health. This time Elis came to the door. No way was he going to accept gifts from Norman. Talk about pride—these two were a right pair. He had given Norman the gift of healing. That put him one up. If he accepted Norman's gifts, Norman would draw level. No way! One chink of light. Norman decided to become a devotee of Elis' God, but this presented him with a problem. He would have to go with his king into the Temple of Rimmon to worship as part of his duty as a court official. 'Will God forgive me?', he asks Elis. For the first time Elis bends. 'Go in peace', he says to Norman. It has entered into Elis' experience and thought, perhaps for the first time, that in this life compromises have to be made now and then, and sometimes risks have to be taken.

Two pairs of people. The first pair had no difficulty in their relationship because the labels that society puts on people didn't matter to them. They were free to give, they were free to accept, without pride, without embarrassment, without a sense of the need to match present with present. They had so little time to develop their friendship, but it was such a precious gift from God, they were determined to make the most of it and not waste time with silly inhibitions.

The second pair had no chance of being close, life-long friends. They were much too devoted to keeping up appearances. They loved their labels and clung to them.

Tragic therefore that whereas Norman recovered from the virus that threatened to put an end to his life, Jonathan succumbed to a different virus.

All life-destroying viruses must be taken seriously. AIDS was not taken seriously at the beginning. A few gay people less would be a good thing. Some actually said it, many more thought it. There might well be a cure and a vaccine by now if the virus had struck the straight community first in the West. It is still not taken seriously enough. In the name of God, aren't the figures from Africa serious enough? Again, what would be the response of our governments if what is happening in Africa were happening here in Europe or in the States? A bit more urgency and a bit more haste, I think.

But we must never forget that AIDS is not the only virus, nor the only cause of an early death. Jonathan died on the field of battle, and David wrote one of the most beautiful poems in human history. War is a virus. How seriously do we take the need to combat that virus? Prejudice is a virus—people are still dying as a result of racism and homophobia. Ignorance is a virus—the unwillingness to face problems and issues rationally and with an open mind

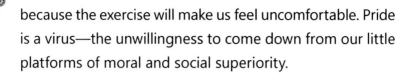

because the exercise will make us feel uncomfortable. Pride is a virus—the unwillingness to come down from our little platforms of moral and social superiority.

Jesus said, 'I have come that you may have life—life in all its fullness'. Let's work harder in the sight of God and humanity to rid this world of every virus that threatens the life in all its fullness that Jesus proclaimed.

Chapter 13

THE BIG PARTY

Ray Vincent

Luke 14:15-24.

God is the great present-giver. God gives us all we have—life, food, clothing, shelter. The story of Christmas is part of the story of how God gives us salvation and eternal life. This too is a gift. We do not earn it by striving to be good. Our friendship with God, all the gifts of the Holy Spirit, the promise of the Kingdom, life more abundant here and now—all are free. We are invited to a feast free of charge—a great eternal Christmas party.

Jesus told a story about a feast. It was in response to a rather pious listener who called out 'How blessed are those who will sit down to the feast in the Kingdom of God!' The person who made that remark was probably thinking of the teaching that was common among the rabbis at that time and is still popular among religious people today—the teaching that those who are good and pious, living upright lives, will go to heaven, while those who have not been so good, who have not said their prayers and led upright lives, will be excluded and punished.

But the story Jesus told turns all that on its head. A man was giving a great feast. The invitations had been sent out in advance, but now it was time for the guests to come. The custom in those days was to send out servants (the 'callers') at the last moment to tell the guests the meal was ready. They didn't have telephones to do it in those days! But by this time all the guests had cried off. One had just bought a piece of land and was going to survey it. Another had bought some farm animals and wanted to try them out. Another had just got married. So what did the host do? He sent his 'callers' around the streets and back alleys to invite anybody they saw—poor people, disabled people, blind people . . . in other words, all the beggars. After that, there was still room, so he sent them out again to go further, out into the country lanes, and he said, 'Do your best to get them to come. I'm determined to have a houseful!' That, says Jesus, is the true nature of the great feast of the kingdom—not an exclusive thing for the deserving, but a free-for-all, an invitation from a sociable God who loves to have a full house!

A lot of what we say about the Church, in our official statements and so on, sounds very solemn. It sounds as if it's meant for serious minded people who read the Bible a lot and can understand theology, and who live a very careful life to make sure they don't do anything wrong. But

Jesus talked about the kingdom as a feast. It's an invitation to join a party! And it's an open party. Anyone can come! God wants a full house!

Unfortunately the Church has often fallen back into the Pharisees' way of thinking. Only the respectable, the pious and the deserving may come. And when they come they look around them at hundreds of empty pews and moan because the others don't come! We don't stop to ask what it is about us that makes people feel unwelcome. The church, in most places, hardly lives up to this image of a feast.

But what about eternal salvation itself? Jesus ended the story with the host saying, 'Those on my original list who turned down my invitation will miss the most exciting event of all time!' In other words, those you would expect to be there won't be there! Somehow they have missed out on it. Why? Because a free gift, by definition, does have one condition. You have to believe in it and accept it!

We have become a bit hardened today to 'free gifts'. We get so many offers from shops and finance companies that we instinctively look for the catch. I once had a phone call telling me I had been selected for a free holiday in Spain. What happened next was so time-consuming and such an anti-climax that I now ignore all such offers. We hesitate to accept a gift from a stranger because we can't really believe that anybody would just give something away. It is surprisingly difficult to give anything away—as a friend and I found one night when we had two concert tickets to spare and offered them to people waiting in the queue. We must have offered them to about twenty people before someone accepted them!

The other condition of a generous free gift is that it usually confronts us with a choice. In order to take advantage of it we may have to change our plans and re-think our priorities. The people who can really join in the party of the Kingdom are those who are prepared to make it a priority. This doesn't mean being in church every Sunday. If we think that, we are turning it back into something pious again! Look again at the story. What were the excuses, the things that came first, for those people? Not vice, or laziness, or worldly pleasures. There were three excuses. The one who had just bought a field was preoccupied with his property. The one who had bought some farm animals was concerned about work and business. The one who had just got married had to make the responsibilities of marriage his first priority. It wasn't their pleasures, it was their responsibilities that kept them away from the party.

Property, work and marriage—the three fundamental constituents of respectable society. And these, Jesus implies, are the three things most likely to keep people out of the Kingdom! Property is all very well: most of us have it, and it entails responsibilities. But if we want to join the feast of God's kingdom we must realise that the earth belongs to God, not to us, and it is meant for all God's creatures to enjoy. Work is very necessary, and so is the money we earn by it. But if we want to join the feast we have to see the vision of a sharing world where people are more important than money: first things first! Marriage is good, and family life is necessary. But if we want to belong to God's kingdom we have to see that no relationships can be exclusive and inward-looking. In God's world, we love everybody. It is not a lot of little families minding their own business, but one big family.

The good news of Jesus is an invitation to a bigger, better life, a life in God's great party!

Here is an adaptation of an old Sankey hymn (Sacred Songs & Solos, number 405):

Come, for everything's ready, all the tables are laid.
It's a free invitation, so don't be afraid.
There is food here in plenty and the choicest of wine,
and God's sent out the message, 'Come in now and dine'.

> ***Come and join in the party,***
> ***Come from near and from far!***
> ***God would love you to be there, whoever you are.***

We are sometimes too busy with our worries and care,
with jobs and with houses, not a moment to spare.

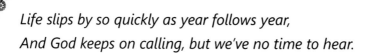

Life slips by so quickly as year follows year,
And God keeps on calling, but we've no time to hear.

There are others God calls in their hunger and need,
but we keep them out with our self-serving greed.
We grab the top places and the best of the fare,
but the food will just choke us till we learn how to share.

So let's go for the real feast for ourselves and for all,
and let the world know of God's wide open call.
Go out on the highways and invite them all in,
till the house has been filled and the party can swing!

Chapter 14

WRAPPED IN FLESH

John Henson
(Christmas Eve, Midnight Communion)

'Wrapped in flesh the Godhead see' is what Charles Wesley wrote in his great Christmas hymn. Someone thought that Wesley's words were indelicate. We should not think of God as a parcel. So whoever it was amended Wesley's words to 'veiled in flesh', and that's how it stands in most hymnbooks. Often we do have to revise hymns to make them more suitable for changed times and ways of thinking. It must have been a Victorian who brought in the veil. Some Victorians, we are told, thought it indecent even to expose the legs of chairs and tables and so put covers on them. We've moved on since then. The picture Wesley was trying to paint in his poetry was not of something needing to be hidden, like a female royal seeking to hide the grief of mourning. No, Wesley wanted us to imagine a present wrapped in attractive paper or packaging, inviting the recipient to open it and reveal its contents. God's parcel? Yes, says Wesley. That's the true meaning of Christmas. God's present has arrived, just like the presents we receive through the post or are handed to us by our friends, or are put round in the tree or in our stockings. We all like to get presents. Well, here it is, God's present, carefully, artistically, intriguingly wrapped. 'Wrapped in flesh'.

Does the wrapping matter? It used to matter to my mother. My mother was a Welsh 'Mam'. She used to say that she allowed my father to make all the important decisions. That left her with all the decisions that she deemed less important, like where we were to go on holiday, or what shirt and tie my father would wear each day. She also ruled all the rituals at Christmas. Apart from the stockings filled by Santa Claus, my father and I and whoever was staying with us over Christmas were allowed to open one present each at the breakfast table. No other presents were to be opened until after the Christmas mid-day meal. Then the assembled company would sit around the tree and we were handed our presents. Mam would invite us one by one to open a present, so that we each watched each other as we unwrapped our parcels. No one was allowed to jump their turn, and no one was allowed to guess what was in a parcel. It had to be a surprise up to the last minute. This is where my father would mischievously step out of line and receive a sharp rebuke. We all had to be terribly careful not to tear the paper. Presents were tied with string in those days. You were handed a pair of scissors, but if possible you untied the knots, opened the wrapping paper and expressed your surprise and joy at your present, even if it were only a pair of socks. Mam would then collect your string and the paper which she folded neatly and put it into a box, to be used again next Christmas. The time I speak of was just after the 1939-45 war.

The wrapping **is** important. If someone just hands you a Tesco bag and says, 'Your present's in there', somehow it's not the same. The wrapping represents thought and care—perhaps not very much, but some. The wrapping was very important at the first Christmas. God's present was wrapped in flesh. God gave us a present in the most beautiful, attractive wrapping imaginable. That is what God thinks of human flesh. The Church has tragically sought to teach otherwise—to predispose us to think that flesh = bad, and that only spirit is good. It has given us fears and hang-ups so that flesh alternately intrigues and disgusts. God's packaging which has the stamp of God's approval and in which God takes pride as a work of art, we turn into an object of lust. The Incarnation, God's wrapping of flesh, is God's way of saying that flesh is O.K.; our humanity is O.K.; it's God's chosen way of presentation. Not just the baby. The child becomes an adult. Children are beautiful; adults are beautiful; not to exploit and degrade, but to value and treasure and care for. Why do humans, including Christians, behave so badly towards one other? Because we do not see one another as God sees us. What God has made God loves and what God has made is good.

Inside the wrapping is the present. The present is God. 'Wrapped in flesh the Godhead see' 'Hail, the Incarnate Deity'. God's present of himself—Father, Mother, Friend;

Life, Love, Hope; Beauty, Goodness, Truth;—that is what you and everyone else is offered this and every Christmas; from the Archbishop of Canterbury to the imprisoned child murderer Ian Huntley; from the Pope to the terrorist; from Her Majesty the Queen to the drunk sleeping in the shop doorway. That's it! No one needs to be without God; no one needs to be without all that God is and God brings. Yet with all the gifts we give and receive each Christmas, and with all the frustrations we have at the things we would like to have and can't have, we either miss God's gift or crazily undervalue it.

A gift has to be unwrapped. That's where each of us comes in as an individual. God is on offer to the world. In one sense we cannot selfishly hold on to the gift for ourselves. It is a parcel to be passed on, like a musical parcel. All the same, we each have our turn to unwrap it. No one can do it for us. And each one of us as we unwrap the parcel will do it in our own way and have our own experience of discovery and joy, which may be quite different from that of the next person. Have you ever received a gift and left it unopened? I have a vague memory of having mislaid a Christmas present and coming across it half way through the year. I can't remember what it was or who it was from. I've got a feeling it might have been money. It's not a thing we normally do. Even if we don't expect that much from the parcel, even if we don't think much of the one who has given it to us, we do the present the justice of opening it up. Someone has gone to the trouble of wrapping it, so we will go to the trouble of opening it. And we may get a nice surprise.

God's present remains so often unopened, even hidden out of sight, forgotten. The lovely man who once walked the dusty roads of Palestine, showing to people the true nature of God, which is Love—that man can be found in our world today and still shows us how God is Love and offers to us the present of God's very self. Will you accept God's present this Christmas? I won't tell you how to unwrap it. You can unwrap it your own way. You can explore the mystery for yourself.

Lightning Source UK Ltd.
Milton Keynes UK
UKOW04f2328150615

253546UK00001B/44/P